ALGERIA
in Pictures

Francesca Davis DiPiazza

TF
CB
Twenty-First Century Books

Contents

Twenty-First Century Books
A division of Lerner Publishing Group, Inc.
241 First Avenue North
Minneapolis, MN 55401 U.S.A.

Website address: www.lernerbooks.com

web enhanced @ www.vgsbooks.com

CULTURAL LIFE 48

► Religion. Holidays. The Arts. Literature. Film and Media. Music. Sports and Recreation. Food.

THE ECONOMY 58

► Industry. Hydrocarbons and Energy. Services and Tourism. Agriculture, Fishing, and Forestry. Transportation and Communication. Trade. The Future.

FOR MORE INFORMATION

Library of Congress Cataloging-in-Publication Data

DiPiazza, Francesca, 1961–
    Algeria in pictures / by Francesca Davis DiPiazza.
        p.   cm. – (Visual geography series)
    Includes bibliographical references and index.
    ISBN: 978-0-8225-7144-5 (lib. bdg. : alk. paper)
    1. Algeria—Pictorial works—Juvenile literature. I. Title.
DT276.D56 2008
965—dc22   2006035004

Manufactured in the United States of America
1 2 3 4 5 6 – PA – 13 12 11 10 09 08

INTRODUCTION

Algeria is a land of striking diversity. Situated in North Africa, the country stretches from the Mediterranean Sea in the north into the Sahara, the world's largest desert. Algeria's population of 33 million people benefits from fertile land along the coast, where most Algerians live. Here groves of olive, fig, and almond trees blossom in spring. The desert, however, covers 80 percent of Algeria's land. Few people live in this parched land except around oases, where underground water comes near the surface. Some groups travel the desert with their herds of animals. The desert may appear barren, but underground it holds the riches that fuel most of Algeria's economy: oil and natural gas.

Through most of its history, Algeria has seen many different groups rise to power—and fall again. The land's earliest inhabitants were wandering herders and hunters. Berber people arrived about five thousand years ago. Over the centuries, conquerors from the Middle East and Europe—Phoenicians, Romans, Byzantines, and Vandals—followed one another. The Romans called the native people Berbers, from the

Romans' word *barbarus*, which means "barbarian." The Berbers called themselves Imazighen, which means "Free People." Settlers established trading posts along the coast. Gradually they pushed the Berbers into the mountains and the south, where they fiercely maintained their independence. The Berbers controlled trade routes linking Algeria with Africa south of the Sahara.

Forces from present-day Saudi Arabia invaded North Africa in the seventh century A.D. The Arabs brought their religion—Islam—to Algeria. The Arabic language also spread throughout the land. For centuries after the Arab conquest, various rival groups controlled different parts of Algeria.

In the sixteenth century, the Ottoman Empire (based in modern Turkey) gained control of Algeria's coast. Under Ottoman rule, Algeria's coastal cities became safe harbors for pirates. These expert sailors robbed ships on the high seas. By the 1800s, piracy had brought several nations into conflict with Algeria.

ATLANTIC
OCEAN

Western Sahara
(Occupied by
MOROCCO)

■ Sahrawi
Refugee Camps

MOROCCO

MAURITANIA

MALI

NIGER

LIBYA

SPAIN

Mediterranean Sea

Tlemcen
Oran
Muaskar•
•Relizane
Tiaret
•Ain Sefra
Cherchell•
Tipasa•
Algiers ⊕
Bejaia•
Sétif•
Constantine
Annaba
Dréan•
Tingad
Tel Kala
Nat'l Park
Carthage
•Biskra
El-Oued•
Hassi Messaoud
Oil Field

Trans-Saharan
Highway

•Tamanrasset

Tassili N'Ajjer
National
Park

TUNISIA

ITALY

Algeria

International border
Trans-Saharan Highway
⊕ Capital city
• City
∴ Ruins

0   200 Miles

0   200 KM

N

INDIAN
OCEAN

FRANCE
ALGERIA
A F R I C A
Gulf of
Guinea

ATLANTIC
OCEAN

0   1000 Miles
0   1000 KM

In 1830 French forces invaded Algiers, the capital of modern Algeria. Soon Algeria became part of France. The French built new industries and roads in Algeria. Colonists arrived from France, Italy, and Spain. These settlers took the best land from the native Algerians and denied Muslims (followers of Islam) any role in Algeria's government. This situation led to a bloody war for independence, beginning in 1954. Algeria won its independence from France in 1962.

The National Liberation Front (FLN, its French initials), the leading pro-independence faction in the war, took over the Algerian government. The FLN made other political parties illegal. The government also tightly controlled the economy.

Support for the FLN began to wane in the 1980s, after many years of economic decline. Conservative Muslim groups gained popularity. They offered strict Islamic law as a solution to the rise in poverty, crime, and corruption.

Under pressure, the FLN finally allowed other parties to run for office in 1991. It looked certain that a radical Islamic party would win the elections and make Algeria an Islamic state. Rather than allow this, the military canceled the elections and outlawed the party. These events led to a civil war that racked the nation throughout the 1990s.

Algeria emerged from the worst of the war in 2000. Small groups of rebels still used terror tactics in remote rural areas. Meanwhile, tensions flared between Algeria's Berber minority and the government. In the face of violent protests, the government granted Berbers more rights.

In the twenty-first century, the growth of Algeria's oil industry has gradually improved the economy. President Bouteflika's landslide reelection in April 2004 reflects his success in bringing some stability to the country. In 2006 the government offered a legal pardon for rebels willing to stop fighting. The nation's hopes for peace have not entirely been met. Not all fighters have put down their arms. Meanwhile, unemployment remains very high, especially among young people. In this unstable environment, Algerians continue to debate the role Islam and democracy should play in their country.

THE LAND

Algeria lies in northwest Africa. It is part of an area known as the Maghreb (meaning "the place where the sun sets" in Arabic, the official language of Algeria). The Mediterranean Sea forms the country's northern coast. Starting at the northeast and moving clockwise, Algeria's neighbors are Tunisia, Libya, Niger, Mali, Mauritania, Western Sahara, and Morocco. Morocco occupies and claims Western Sahara. Spain and France lie across the Mediterranean.

Algeria is the tenth-largest country in the world and the second largest in Africa, after Sudan. Algeria covers an area of 919,595 square miles (2,381,740 square kilometers). The country is almost as big as the United States east of the Mississippi River.

Algeria's 750-mile (1,207 km) Mediterranean coastline was the site of the region's first ports and trading settlements. Small, rocky islands off its northern shores inspired Algeria's name. The name comes from *al-Jazair*, meaning "the islands" in Arabic. Under French rule, Europeans built new houses, roads, and industries in the northern

cities. Most towns, farms, and factories still lie on or near the coast. The Algerian interior consists of mountains, basins (low, flat regions), high plateaus, and part of the hot, dry Sahara.

Topography

The Tell is Algeria's northernmost region. It extends inland 80 to 200 miles (129 to 322 km) all along the Mediterranean coast. *Tell* is Arabic for "hill." In the Tell, rolling hills and narrow plains lie between the sea and the mountains. Short river valleys in these highlands contain fertile soil. Olive and fruit groves, grape vineyards, and wheat fields flourish here.

The Tell also includes mountains. The Tell Atlas range spans northern Algeria as far east as Tunisia. It is an extension of the Atlas Mountains of Morocco. Between the mountains are dry basins, fertile valleys, and plains. The Kabylia Mountains rise south and east of Algiers. The Kabylia area is the heartland of the Berber people. The

The **Aurès Mountains** in northeastern Algeria are taller than the Tell Atlas mountain range to the west.

Medjerda range, east of the city of Constantine, runs northeastward across the Tunisian border. The entire Atlas mountain system is prone to earthquakes.

South of the Tell region are the rolling plains of the High Plateau region. This land varies from 1,300 to 4,300 feet (396 to 1,311 meters) in elevation. Herders graze goats, sheep, and camels on the dry land here. To the south and west, these plains rise gradually to the Saharan Atlas Mountains. Higher than the Tell Atlas, the Saharan Atlas Mountains run from the Moroccan border to the Algerian desert town of Biskra.

The High Plateau region contains many flat salt basins called *chotts*. The chotts fill up with water and become salty marshes during the region's rare rains. Chott Melrhir, near the Tunisian border, reaches Algeria's lowest elevation—102 feet (31 m) below sea level. Just north of Chott Melrhir are the Aurès Mountains. They receive occasional snowfalls during Algeria's short winter.

The Algerian Sahara region begins south of the Saharan Atlas. Lying in the northern Sahara are the Great Western and Great Eastern *ergs*. Ergs are vast regions of sand dunes. Also in the area is the Mzab, a rocky limestone plateau. Iguidi Erg and Chech Erg straddle the Mauritanian and Malian borders, respectively. Desert oases—small, fertile areas that draw their water from underground—are scattered throughout the Sahara. With limited water and little fertile soil, the southern Sahara supports only a few small towns. The independent

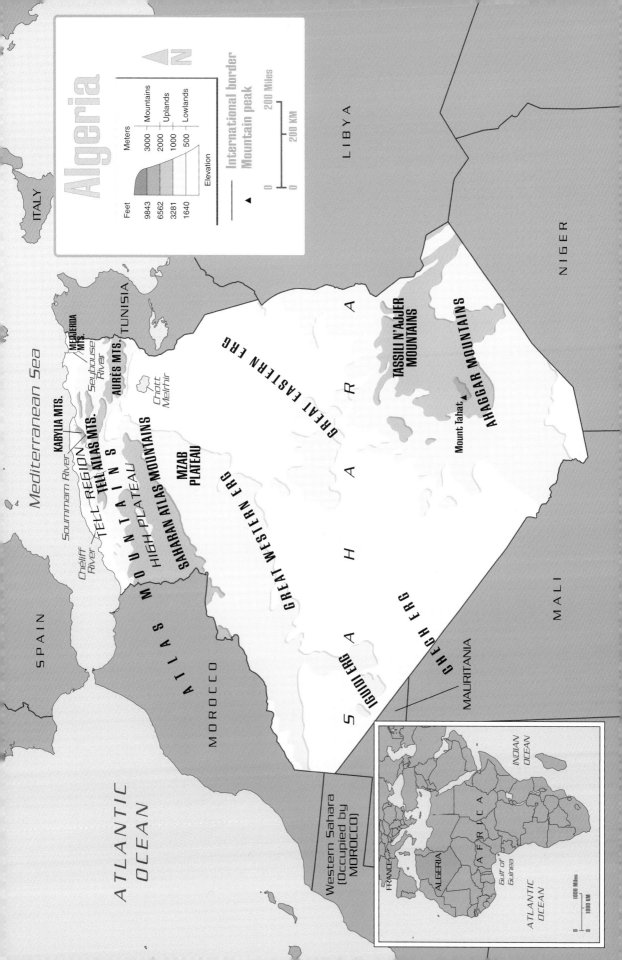

Algeria

Elevation

Feet	Meters	
9843	3000	Mountains
6562	2000	Uplands
3281	1000	Lowlands
1640	500	

International border
▲ Mountain peak

200 Miles
200 KM
0

ITALY

Mediterranean Sea

SPAIN

ATLANTIC OCEAN

MOROCCO

Western Sahara (Occupied by MOROCCO)

TUNISIA

LIBYA

NIGER

MALI

MAURITANIA

KABYLIA MTS.
MEDJERDA MTS.
Seybouse River
Soummam River
Chéliff River
TELL REGION
TELL ATLAS MTS.
AURÈS MTS.
Chott Melrhir
HIGH PLATEAU
SAHARAN ATLAS MOUNTAINS
MZAB PLATEAU
ATLAS MOUNTAINS
S A H A R A
GREAT WESTERN ERG
GREAT EASTERN ERG
IGUIDI ERG
CHECH ERG
TASSILI N'AJJER MOUNTAINS
AHAGGAR MOUNTAINS
Mount Tahat ▲

FRANCE
AFRICA
ALGERIA
Gulf of Guinea
ATLANTIC OCEAN
INDIAN OCEAN

1000 Miles
1000 KM
0

THE GREEN SAHARA

Sahara means "desert" in Arabic. The Sahara covers an area as large as the United States. About ten thousand years ago—during the last ice age—the Sahara was a green and fertile land. Gradually the climate changed, and plant and animal life dwindled. However, some water from the era remains. This "fossil water" accumulated in aquifers—natural rock chambers deep underground. Algerians dig wells to reach the water.

Berber people here depend on oases and deep wells for their survival in the desert. The Tuareg— a proud Berber people—travel with their herds in search of grazing land and water. Most roads in the region are bumpy tracks. The desert's shifting sands often bury them.

The Tassili N'Ajjer Mountains, a remote range in southeastern Algeria, rise near Libya. Volcanic activity helped form the Ahaggar Mountains farther south. They include Mount Tahat. At 9,852 feet (3,003 m) above sea level, this is the highest point in Algeria. Erosion of volcanic rocks in the Ahaggar has created a moonlike landscape.

This **erg, or vast region of sand dunes,** lies in the northern Sahara.

Rivers

Algeria has limited water resources and no rivers big enough for boats to travel on. Most streams in the Tell region run northward through narrow mountain passes. They empty into the Mediterranean Sea. Dams on some of these waterways create reservoirs that provide irrigation (artificial watering systems) for farms.

The 450-mile (724 km) Chéliff River is the country's longest waterway. Rising in the Tell Atlas south of Algiers, the Chéliff turns sharply westward. It empties into the Mediterranean, east of the port of Oran. Separating the Great Kabylia and Little Kabylia ranges, the Soummam River reaches the Mediterranean near the harbor town of Bejaïa. The Seybouse River is 145 miles (233 km) long. It originates in the Medjerda range and waters a level plain south of Annaba, a busy port city.

No permanent rivers exist south of the Tell Atlas. During the rainy season in the High Plateau, temporary streams run through wadis (dry valleys). Most of these streams empty into the low-lying, salty chotts. A few small rivers also flow during the rainy season high in the Saharan Atlas. They dry up during the rainless season. Underground sources provide much-needed freshwater in the oases of the Sahara.

Climate

During most of the year, Algeria has a hot and dry climate. Northern winds blow in winter and spring. They bring occasional rainfall. Much of the rain falls on the country's north-facing slopes. The basins and valleys near Algeria's Mediterranean coast have warm, dry summers and mild winters.

In the summer, dust- and sand-laden winds called siroccos sweep across Algeria from the Sahara. These hot, dry blasts of wind can wither plants in a matter of hours. Their grit coats buildings, cars, and streets. Fine dust gets into the eyes, noses, and mouths of people and animals. Siroccos blow for as many as forty days. The scorching winds even carry sand across the Mediterranean Sea to southern Europe.

Annual rainfall in the Tell varies from 16 to 39 inches (41 to 99 centimeters). Droughts, or times of little or no rain, sometimes threaten crops and wildlife here. Summer temperatures in the region average 78°F (26°C). Winters average 50°F (10°C).

Little rain falls on Algeria's south-facing slopes, southern ranges, and interior plateaus. The High Plateau receives a yearly average of 8 to 16 inches (20 to 41 cm) of rain, mostly from September through December. For the rest of the year, drought conditions prevail.

Temperatures in the region average 81°F (27°C) in summer and 40°F (4°C) in winter.

The Sahara experiences extremes in temperature, with very low humidity (moisture in the air). Midday temperatures often reach 120°F (49°C). With no cloud cover to hold the day's heat in, night-time temperatures fall to near freezing. Average annual rainfall in the Sahara is less than 5 inches (13 cm). Some areas receive no rain for years.

Flora and Fauna

Algeria's coastal areas support sparse natural vegetation, such as lavender and wild olive trees. In mountainous and well-watered regions of the Tell, deciduous (leaf-shedding) trees such as oak grow. Atlas cedar and Aleppo pine are also common trees. Woodlands cover less than 1 percent of the country's land.

Esparto grass and brushwood flourish in the flat basins of the High Plateau. Thorny acacia trees, jujube trees, and scrub vegetation grow on the northern plains of the Sahara. South of the Saharan Atlas, plants adapted to dry conditions survive near wadis. Date palms have deep roots to draw underground water in the oases.

Wild boars and a small number of antelope live in Algeria's remote mountainous regions. The highlands are home to Barbary red deer and Barbary sheep, Africa's only wild sheep. ("Barbary" is a former European name for North Africa, based on the word "Berber.") Hares,

Thorny acacia trees and other scrub vegetation are common in Algeria. They manage to survive in the northern plains of the Sahara.

porcupines, and gazelles survive in the Tell. North Africa's only monkey, the macaque, lives in northern Algeria too. It is also called the Barbary ape.

In the desert, people still use camels as a means of transportation. Camels came from Arabia about two thousand years ago. They can survive for two weeks without water. Their tough mouths can chew thorny desert plants. A double row of eyelashes protects their eyes from blowing sand. Camels' padded feet are wide and flat, providing stability on sand like snowshoes do on snow.

Many desert animals are nocturnal, or active at night when it is cool. For instance, the fennec, or desert fox, sleeps in burrows under the hot sand during the day. The temperature 3 feet (0.9 m) below the desert surface stays a steady 75°F (24°C), day and night. At night the fennec's large ears help it locate prey. The thin-skinned ears also help release the fox's body heat, as

Fennec

hot blood circulates through them. Striped hyenas and golden jackals also hunt at night. Predators (animals that hunt other animals) get most of the liquid they need from their prey's body fluids. They feed on the desert's many rodents, including sand rats and jerboas. Long-tailed jerboas jump on their back legs like tiny kangaroos. Snakes, lizards, and scorpions inhabit the Sahara too.

Algeria's mountains are full of birdlife including hawks, owls, vultures, and the lammergeier, a vulture that looks like a huge falcon. The Algerian nuthatch is the only bird that is unique to Algeria. Seabirds include gulls, terns, and cormorants. The Audouin's gull is the only kind of gull that lives only in the Mediterranean. These gulls nest along Algeria's coast in the spring. Birds migrating to and from Europe, including flamingos, also stop over on the coast.

Mediterranean waters are rich in sea life. Fishers catch anchovies, sardines, tuna, and shellfish. A few dozen Mediterranean monk seals live in rocky coastal areas. They are endangered, or threatened with dying out.

Natural Resources and Environmental Issues

Algeria is rich in mineral and energy resources. Large oil and natural gas deposits exist in the Sahara. Large reserves of phosphate, a mineral used in fertilizer, lie near the Tunisian border. Other

Algerian minerals include iron ore, coal, lead, zinc, and mercury. These materials are valuable in manufacturing and as exports. Deposits of uranium, used to generate nuclear energy, lie near Tamanrasset in the south.

Fertile land in the coastal region produces grains, olives, and fruit. The country's limited forests provide hardwood, cork from cork oaks, and rope. Ocean waters support a fishing industry, and coastal ports allow for trade and transportation.

The spread of the Sahara is a major environmental challenge for Algeria. Algeria's land suffers from overcultivation of crops and overgrazing of animals. These farming activities wear out the soil. Deforestation is the removal of trees for timber, fuel, or to create farmland. With the loss of tree roots to anchor it, soil dries up and blows away. These factors lead to desertification—the process of drylands (arid regions) becoming barren desert. Drought increases the rate of desertification.

Algeria lacks enough water for its people, industries, and farms. In response, the U.S.-based General Electric Company is building Africa's largest desalination plant in Algeria. Desalination is an expensive process that removes salt from seawater, making it safe for people and crops.

Algeria's industries and cities have grown greatly since the 1960s. Their growth helps the country's economy but creates pollution. Waste from Algeria's oil industry and oil tankers (ships) pollutes the Mediterranean Sea. Industrial waste, fertilizer runoff, and raw sewage pollute rivers and coastal waters. Because of pollution and loss of habitat, thirty-two animal species in Algeria are endangered.

WORLD ENVIRONMENT DAY

Algeria hosted the annual international World Environment Day in 2006. The day focused on the spread of deserts, and the slogan was Don't Desert Drylands! Citizens planted trees, held marches, and taught about the environment in schools. President Bouteflika of Algeria urged world leaders to adopt a World Charter on Deserts—a plan to help stop desertification.

Studies done by the United Nations (an international organization for peace and development) show that desert covers almost 25 percent of the world's land. The percentage is growing. Former UN leader Kofi Annan warned, "Across the planet, poverty, unsustainable land management and climate change are turning drylands into deserts, and desertification in turn . . . leads to poverty. . . ."

The Algerian government tries to balance the needs of its people and the needs of the environment. Protected areas such as El Kala National Park aid the survival of some of Algeria's wildlife. Government-sponsored tree planting programs in Algerian highlands have reduced soil erosion. The government's 2002 National Environmental Action Plan focuses on providing sanitation and clean drinking water, fighting deforestation, and saving plants and animals. It has had some success in meeting these goals.

Cities

Like many North African cities, Algeria's modern cities grew outward from a central medina, or old part of town. Medinas feature souks (covered outdoor markets) where merchants offer crafts, fresh fruits and vegetables, colorful mounds of spices, and even live animals.

Algeria's largest cities are along or near the Mediterranean coastline. Trade and industry thrive near these cities' ports. From the port cities, companies export raw materials, oil, natural gas, and finished goods. Smaller cities of the interior developed near water sources and along ancient trade routes.

Algeria's capital city, Algiers, is on the coast of the Mediterranean Sea. The white buildings of the old quarter gave the city the nickname Algiers the White.

Many people from poor rural areas have moved to the northern cities in search of jobs and housing. The result has been overcrowding, since 59 percent of Algeria's population lives in cities. Unemployment is high too, especially among young people. It has led to the development of a new word: *hitiste*. The word is an Arabic-French mix that means "one who holds up walls." It describes a young man with nothing to do but hang around, leaning against buildings.

ALGIERS is Algeria's capital and largest city. About 3 million people live in the city and its suburbs. Phoenician traders (from modern Lebanon) first settled the city on the Mediterranean Sea. Algiers later was home to Romans from the Italian peninsula and Berbers from the Sahara. From the 1400s until the 1800s, pirates sailed from Algiers's harbor. In the 1830s, the city came under French control. During the 1950s, Algiers's mazelike medina was the center of resistance against the French.

Government offices, museums, and palm trees line wide boulevards near Algiers's harbor. The city streets become narrow, winding alleys in the old casbah quarter. A ruined fortress, or casbah, is a feature of this medina. The white buildings of the quarter rise steeply above the harbor. They glisten in the sun, earning the city the nickname Algiers the White.

Algiers's main industries are oil refining, metalworking, and food and petrochemicals processing. The city is an important Mediter-ranean seaport. It is also the hub of Algeria's air, rail, and road networks.

ORAN (population 1 million) sits on high cliffs above a wide harbor west of Algiers. First settled in the tenth century, Oran came under Spanish rule in the 1500s. The city was rebuilt after a devastating earthquake in 1790. Under French occupation, European architects and engineers designed elegant houses and tree-lined boulevards in the city's center.

Modern Oran exports produce—including wine, grains, fruit, and vegetables. Many West African nations ship their goods through Oran's port. The city's harbor also contains facilities for shipbuilding and ship repair. Factories make carpets, textiles, beverages, and machinery.

CONSTANTINE (population 800,000) was built on a rocky hilltop. It was once the city of Cirta, the capital of Numidia, an ancient Berber kingdom. In A.D. 313, Romans renamed the settlement after a Roman

The city of Constantine features many bridges, including the Peregaux Bridge, stretching across a river gorge. Constantine is built on a plateau high above sea level. Visit www.vgsbooks.com for links to websites with more photos of Algeria's cities and villages.

emperor. Constantine came under French control in 1837. A modern section of wide streets and colonial buildings surrounds Constantine's small medina. The city's major industries make leather and cloth goods.

ANNABA (population 250,000) is a busy port, northeast of Constantine. The city began as Hippo Regius, a Roman settlement. The elaborate ruins of the old Roman city still attract visitors to Annaba. Exporters ship minerals and agricultural goods from the port. A naval base is also located here.

HISTORY AND GOVERNMENT

Thousands of years ago, the Sahara was a savanna, or grassland, where ample rain fell. In the Tassili N'Ajjer Mountains in southeastern Algeria, thousands of paintings and carvings on rock show humans hunting wild animals, such as giraffes, on the savanna. The earliest art is up to ten thousand years old. Later rock art illustrates crops and domesticated animals, such as cattle. Images include 8-foot (2.4 m) tall floating human figures, possibly depicting religious experiences.

By 4000 B.C., a climate change was taking place. Rainfall lessened, and the land turned to desert. The inhabitants gradually moved to more fertile areas. In northern Algeria, the migrating hunters and farmers met and intermarried with a group of newcomers whose exact origins are unknown. Europeans later called these people Berbers.

The Berbers spoke a common language. Their society was made up of many independent clans (groups of families). They lived as nomads—people who move from place to place in search of grazing

lands and water. The clans often combined into larger groups. Some Berber groups established control over large areas of North Africa. Few ancient Berber leaders, however, established lasting states in Algeria.

About 1200 B.C., Phoenician seafarers and traders from the Middle East began to build outposts along Africa's Mediterranean coast. These merchants soon began trading with the Berbers.

In 814 B.C., the Phoenicians founded Carthage on the coast of present-day Tunisia. Carthage's name means "new city" in Punic, the Phoenician language. Carthage became North Africa's wealthiest city. With a large merchant navy, the Carthaginian Empire eventually gained control over much of the Mediterranean coast. Carthaginians and Berbers worked together to protect their trade networks. The Carthaginians paid Berber soldiers to defend their cities against raiders. By the third century B.C., Carthage was coming under attack by the armies of Rome, a republic based in Italy.

Roman Rule

The conflict between Rome and Carthage turned into a series of three wars called the Punic Wars, beginning in 264 B.C. A Berber leader, Masinissa, switched his loyalty to Rome. Masinissa took charge of the Berber kingdom of Numidia about 200 B.C. He established his capital at Cirta (modern Constantine) and expanded his kingdom along the coast. After battling in both Europe and Africa, Rome finally defeated the Carthaginians in 146 B.C. The victors destroyed the city of Carthage and built new Roman cities along the coast.

> Phoenicians brought their religious beliefs to North Africa. They worshipped many gods. Eshmun was the Phoenician god of wealth and health. His name means "to be fat." And Phoenician cities in North Africa did grow large and rich, mostly through trade in gold, ivory, and slaves from West Africa.

After Masinissa's death, his heirs continued to rule Numidia. Masinissa's grandson Jugurtha carried out a long campaign against Roman armies. Rome defeated Jugurtha's forces in 105 B.C. and made Numidia part of its North African territory. Romans divided their territory into provinces. Military governors ruled the provinces.

After the defeat of Jugurtha, Roman settlers built towns and large farms in the region. The inhabitants spoke Latin—Rome's language. Aqueducts (structures to transport water) and roads helped trade and agriculture to flourish. Berber farmers rented land from the Romans. They paid their rent with grain. The Romans built ports to ship the region's large harvests to Italy. Eventually Numidia was supplying much of Rome's grain.

For several centuries, Numidia remained a prosperous Roman province. Yet events in other parts of the Roman Empire affected the region. Conflict with peoples living near the Roman frontiers in Europe weakened the empire's defenses. In addition, Christianity—a religion from the Roman province of Palestine (modern Israel)—gained Berber followers. Many of the new Christians in North Africa joined a growing movement for independence from Rome.

Vandal Invasions

In the early A.D. 300s, the Roman emperor Constantine made Christianity Rome's official religion. But the independence movement in Numidia against Roman rule remained strong. More importantly, Rome's African lands were vulnerable to attack from outsiders. In 429 the Vandals—a Germanic group—crossed from Spain and invaded

Ruins of the Roman city of Timgad can be found near the Aurès Mountains
in Algeria. Berbers destroyed the city in the seventh century, and over time
the desert sands buried the buildings, leaving them amazingly preserved.
The ruins include a library, four bathhouses, and an open-air theater. The
theater is in such good shape that performances are still held there.

North Africa. They quickly overran much of Numidia. Vandal leaders
allowed Roman officials to continue to run Numidia. But Roman military power was declining, and much of the region fell into disorder.

Meanwhile, Berber nomads south of the Tell set up new trade
routes across the Sahara. They controlled the valuable trade in gold,
ivory, salt, and slaves across the desert. (Slavery was common in much
of the world and had been since ancient times.) Merchants traveled
across the desert in groups called caravans, with camels carrying goods
and supplies.

The Vandals held the coast of North Africa until the early sixth
century. At that time, Byzantine forces from eastern Europe arrived.
They took control of North African ports. Byzantine rule in Algeria
lasted only until the mid-seventh century. It ended when Arabs from
present-day Saudi Arabia invaded North Africa.

The Arab Conquest and Berber Dynasties

The invading Arabs were Muslims who brought Islam, a new religion,
to Algeria. Muslims believe that Allah ("God" in Arabic) gave his final
teachings to the Arab prophet (spiritual messenger) Muhammad. In the
century following Muhammad's death in 632, Muslim Arabs conquered most of North Africa. Some inhabitants of Algeria fought

BERBER QUEEN

During the Arab conquest, Berber leader Queen Dihya led her troops against the invading warriors in the Aurès region. In 702 Arab warriors cut off her head and sent it back to Arabia as proof of her defeat. The heroic queen entered Algerian legend as La Kahena (the Prophetess).

against the Arab invaders. Others accepted the new rulers and converted to Islam. In certain regions, such as in the Kabylia and Aurès mountains, Berber clans accepted Islam but held on to self-rule.

In the eighth century, North Africa came under the control of the Abbasid dynasty (family of rulers). Based in Baghdad (in modern Iraq), the Abbasids conquered much of North Africa and Spain. They called their domain the Maghreb, signifying it was in the west. The Maghreb encompassed present-day Morocco, Algeria, Tunisia, and northwestern Libya.

Abbasid control of the Algerian seacoast provided security for the region's port towns. Trade with the Middle East and Europe remained active. Arabic-speaking merchants on the coast formed partnerships with the Berbers of the interior. Trade and religion gradually spread the Arabic language to Berbers throughout the land.

Not all Berber clans accepted Arab rule or the traditional form of Islam. Several Berber kingdoms had established nontraditional sects of Islam. These kingdoms rose to oppose Abbasid rule. The Rustimid dynasty ruled a Berber kingdom based at Tahart (modern Tiaret). This dynasty became one of the most powerful of these Berber realms.

Camel caravans, such as this one in Algeria in the late 1800s, transported goods in the region.

Tahart controlled many caravan routes. Trade in gold and grain brought riches, and the city became a seat of culture and learning. By the late 700s, the Rustimid Berbers had broken free of Abbasid rule.

In the late 800s, Berbers from the Kabylia region installed a new Arab dynasty, the Fatimids. They took their name from Fatima, the daughter of the prophet Muhammad. The Fatimids conquered Tahart and drove the Rustimid dynasty southward.

The Berbers rebelled against the Fatimids in the late 900s, and Fatimid control weakened. Berber clans switched their loyalties from the Arabs back to local Berber chieftains.

The Bedouin and Arab Brotherhoods

In the eleventh century, the Fatimids attempted to regain control over Algeria. They did so by inviting Arab nomads—known as Bedouin—to migrate to North Africa. The Bedouin devastated cities and farms, forcing many Berbers from their lands. Eventually, however, the new Arabs settled and intermarried with the Berbers.

At this time, new Islamic groups, or brotherhoods, were gaining followers among the Berbers. These brotherhoods rallied around Islamic holy men, who demanded a strict observance of Islamic law. They established semi-military groups. One such group, the Almoravids, gained control of the Maghreb by 1056. In 1086 the Almoravids conquered southern Spain.

In 1144, after a series of victories, the Almohads trapped the Almoravid leader, Tachfine ben Ali, in the port city of Oran. Rather than accept the dishonor of surrender, ben Ali galloped on his horse off a cliff into the sea.

Another group of Berber Islamic reformers was known as the Almohads. Their base was in Morocco. By 1147 the Almohads had taken control from the Almoravids. They became rulers of the Maghreb and southern Spain. This realm supported a flowering of Muslim art and learning. The Almohad center at Tlemcen grew wealthy by controlling Algeria's ports. North Africa became an important source of gold for the European states. The Almohads eventually could not hold their large empire together. By 1269 their Maghreb realm had split into smaller kingdoms.

Ottomans and Pirates

While various Berber dynasties rose and fell from power, Europeans often raided the region's Mediterranean coast. In 1492 Spanish

Christians retook Spain from Muslim rule and forced Muslims and Jews from Spain. The Spanish then conquered several outposts along the African coast, including the Algiers harbor. Muslim and Jewish refugees from Spain began to arrive in other Algerian ports.

Spanish authority in North Africa soon suffered a severe blow. In 1518 the Muslim leader Khayr al-Din became commander of Algiers. Also known as Barbarossa ("Redbeard" in Italian), he placed the city under the control of the Turks of the Ottoman Empire. This huge Muslim realm reached from Asia Minor (modern Turkey) through eastern Europe and the Middle East. Khayr al-Din eventually subdued much of North Africa. He grew wealthy from piracy at sea, with his vessels attacking European merchant ships.

After the death of Khayr al-Din in 1546, the Ottoman Turks took direct control of his realm. They sent Turkish troops to protect the cities and to police the interior. The troops' leader, the *aga*, became the head of government in northern Algeria.

PIRATES

For hundreds of years, Algerian pirates robbed trading ships and took hostages from captured vessels. Some captives became the slaves of merchants and officials in Algiers. Others were held in Algerian prisons until the pirates received a ransom payment. The pirates voyaged as far as the coast of Iceland in search of plunder and prisoners.

Muslim leader Khayr al-Din was known as Barbarossa. He and his brothers became rich through piracy.

The Growth of Algiers

By 1600 Algiers had become the capital of what Europeans called the Barbary Coast. The port city profited from piracy, slave trading, and from ransoms Europeans paid for captives. The many wealthy and powerful pirates formed a guild (alliance) for mutual support. Merchants also exported valuable goods, such as leather and horses, from Algiers.

The Ottoman sultans (leaders) ruled their empire from distant Istanbul (in modern Turkey). They began to lose influence over Algerian affairs. Competition among pirates, traders, and Turkish military leaders made the region unstable. Various southern Berber groups supported competing factions. In 1671 the pirate guild replaced the Ottoman representative in Algiers with a dey (governor). Few deys exercised control beyond Algiers, however. And assassins murdered many of the deys.

In the late 1700s, European states and the United States together took action against the Barbary Coast to end piracy. In 1815 a U.S. force entered the harbor of Algiers and threatened to bomb the city. The dey agreed to end piracy, release all captives, and pay for stolen property. After the dey broke these promises, British and Dutch ships bombed Algiers in 1816 to enforce the agreement. Piracy dwindled but did not come to a complete stop.

French Occupation

Meanwhile, relations between Algiers and its trading partner France were worsening. They disagreed about an old debt, which France refused to pay. In addition, the French government was unpopular at home. The French king, Charles X, sought to increase his popularity by gaining a victory abroad. In 1830 French forces invaded Algiers. Their conquest was popular in France. Four years later, France claimed northern Algeria.

French colons (colonists) moved to Algeria and seized the best farmland in the Tell. The colons' nickname was pieds-noirs, which means "black feet" in French. The name probably comes from the settlers' black shoes. The colons forced many Algerian natives to move to dry southern

In 1827 **Pierre Deval was the French consul (business representative) in Algiers. He ignored Algerian rights and refused to pay France's debts. In a meeting that year, Algiers's dey, Hussein III, grew angry at the consul's arrogance. He flicked Deval with a peacock feather fly whisk (a switch for swatting away flies). French leaders, facing troubles at home, used this insult as one of their excuses to invade Algiers in 1830.**

Abd al-Qadir, whose name means "the Algerian," led a rebellion against French rule in the nineteeth century. The French exiled him from the country. Go to www.vgsbooks.com for links to websites with more information on national heroes in Algeria.

regions. The French foreign legion was an elite group of soldiers equipped for desert warfare. They built forts in Algeria to support and defend the colonists.

In the late 1830s, a movement to resist the French occupation formed around Abd al-Qadir. A popular Muslim leader, Abd al-Qadir established a government at Tlemcen. He and his supporters soon claimed all Algerian territory not directly controlled by French forces.

At first Abd al-Qadir waged an effective guerrilla war (rebellion fought by small bands of fighters). His forces attacked foreign legion outposts and colons' farms. But the French forces destroyed villages and terrorized the native population in return. Many of the guerrillas gave up the fight. Abd al-Qadir surrendered in 1847 and later was forced into exile. Nevertheless, he became the first hero of Algeria's independence movement.

European Settlement

Many settlers from France, Italy, and Spain arrived in Algeria in the mid-1800s. Eventually the European colons took most of Algeria's fertile land, sometimes by force. By 1848 about 100,000 colons and 2.5 million native Algerians lived in Algeria. That year the French government made northern Algeria a part of France. They divided the north into three provinces, with their capitals at Oran, Algiers, and Constantine. The colons ran the French provinces. They built new schools, businesses, and industries. Most colons practiced the Roman

Catholic religion. The French military ran much of Algeria outside the provinces as a colony.

France allowed non-French colons to become citizens of France. But native Algerians could only become citizens in the new French Algeria by accepting French law in place of Islamic law. Few Algerian Muslims were willing to deny their religion to become French citizens.

In 1871 native Algerians revolted against the colons' rule in the Kabylia area. The French put down the rebellion. Afterward, they took native lands in the area. They also placed strict laws on the Muslim inhabitants. By this time, war, disease, and famine had caused the deaths of about one-third of Algeria's native population under French rule.

For the next few decades, an uneasy peace held between European colons and Algerian Muslims. The two groups lived in separate societies. Little communication or intermarriage occurred between them. Colon leaders blocked any Muslim representation in the French legislature (lawmaking body). Colon representatives in France also voted against any laws that would give native Algerians equal rights. The colons controlled Algeria's largest farms, businesses, and its foreign trade.

A few native Algerians became French citizens. They attended universities in France and then returned to Algeria. There they formed a small professional class. Gradually the introduction of modern sanitation and health care increased the population. By the early 1900s, however, the vast majority of Algerian Muslims were poor and uneducated. They were noncitizens in their own land.

World Wars and Muslim Nationalism

In Europe, World War I (1914–1918) broke out when Germany invaded Belgium and France. More than 200,000 Algerian soldiers helped France and its allies defeat Germany.

Algerians who returned home after the war found a divided country. Muslims still lacked job opportunities and the right to vote. Only 10 percent of the native children attended school. Muslim religious leaders called for equality with Europeans in Algeria. Their demands began a wave of nationalism, or an independence movement, among war veterans.

Nationalist leaders formed several groups to press for Algeria's independence from France. The French government responded by proposing laws to let native Algerians become French citizens without losing their Muslim status. But colons in the French legislature blocked reforms.

War once again broke out in Europe. Britain, France, and later the United States allied to oppose Nazi Germany, Italy, and other Axis

Some members of the U.S. military talk with Algerian villagers in November 1942. **U.S. and British troops landed in Algiers and Oran** that month to fight Axis forces in North Africa.

OPERATION TORCH

In November 1942, in a mission called Operation Torch, 107,000 British and U.S. troops landed in Algiers and Oran. The Allies advanced eastward to drive Axis forces out of North Africa. Joined by Free French (non-Vichy) fighters, Allied forces gained all of North Africa by May 1943. The Allies then launched operations across the Mediterranean against enemy-held southern Europe.

nations during World War II (1939–1945). France surrendered after a massive German invasion in 1940. A new French government that cooperated with Germany was set up in the French town of Vichy. The colons were largely in favor of the Vichy government, which also took control of Algeria. Algerian Muslims were not. In 1943 Allied forces defeated pro-Vichy forces and drove the Germans and Italians from North Africa. Algiers served as the Free French capital of France until the Allies freed Paris, the official capital.

During the war, nationalists demanded a new Algerian constitution. But all negotiations with the French government stopped on May 8, 1945—the final day of World War II in Europe. On that day, victory celebrations in Sétif and Constantine turned into anti-European riots. Police fired into the crowds, killing many.

After the riots, many pro-independence leaders called for a revolution. Armed Algerian groups murdered more than one hundred colons. In response, anti-Muslim violence throughout the country killed eight thousand native Algerians. The government arrested and exiled (forced out) nationalist leaders. In Egypt, Algerian leader Ahmed Ben Bella and several other exiled Algerians formed a group that would become the National Liberation Front (known by its French initials, FLN).

The Algerian Revolution

The military branch of the FLN launched a guerrilla war for independence on November 1, 1954. They bombed, assassinated, and ambushed French and colon targets in Algeria. The FLN called on all Muslims to join the revolution. In response, armed colons attacked Muslim villages. They destroyed homes and farms and killed inhabitants.

To counter the violence, the French government sent troops to Algeria. The discovery of oil in the Sahara during the 1950s gave the French added reason to want to keep Algeria. Meanwhile, the independence movement gained a large following.

As violence spread, the French military took drastic measures to put down the revolt. French planes bombed Algerian Muslim towns and villages. Both sides used terror tactics. French forces tortured and humiliated civilians. They forced thousands of Muslims into desert concentration camps. The FLN in turn murdered both colon and Muslim opponents of the independence movement. In the large cities, they placed bombs in cafés and other public places. Women were active in the urban guerrilla war for independence. In the late 1950s, the FLN brought terror tactics to France, with assassinations and bombings there.

General Charles de Gaulle became the new president of France in 1958. A commander of Free French forces during World War II, de Gaulle proved to be a strong leader. In 1959 de Gaulle stated that Algerian Muslims should have the right to elect their own government. Many colons were violently opposed to this position. In response, they formed militias, or private armies. The colon militias carried out brutal attacks both on Muslims and the French armed forces.

Support for the war in Algeria steadily fell in France. International pressure on the French government to settle the conflict increased in the early 1960s. As the war dragged on, French leaders saw that they could not keep control over Algeria or over its majority Muslim population.

Independence and FLN Rule

In March 1962, the French government met with FLN representatives in Evian, Switzerland. The two sides agreed to the right of Algerians to decide their own future. A formal declaration of Algerian independence occurred on July 3, 1962. In September the newly elected legislature proclaimed the founding of the Democratic and Popular Republic of Algeria. Voters elected Ahmed Ben Bella, the founder of the FLN, as the republic's first president, in 1963.

The war had killed about 1 million people, almost one-tenth of the population. Society had been torn apart, with families and villages destroyed. The infrastructure (roads and other public works) also suffered heavy damage. Most colons—about 1 million people—left the country after independence. Algerians who had supported the French became targets of violence. Many of them left too. This emigration drained the country of most of its professional people. The loss included doctors, business owners, and civil servants (government workers).

Algerians faced the difficult task of creating a new country. The FLN passed laws that made it the only legal political party. Ben Bella made Algeria a Socialist state. In a Socialist system, the government

Citizens in Algiers celebrate the country's new **independence from France in July 1962.** Algerians had the tough task ahead of them of rebuilding their country after years of war.

strictly controls the economy. The Algerian government took over businesses, farms, and banks.

An iron-fisted leader, Ben Bella personally controlled the army and the government. He aligned Algeria with the Soviet Union, then a powerful Socialist nation. Some Algerians disagreed with Ben Bella's economic and foreign policies. Houari Boumediene, a hero of the war for independence, was one of them. He gathered other FLN supporters. They overthrew Ben Bella in June 1965.

Ahmed Ben Bella

Boumediene's government canceled the constitution. The new president ruled by personal orders. He focused on improving the economy, hiring skilled people to run state-owned industries. However, the FLN government still did not allow other political organizations. Some Algerians grew frustrated with their lack of democratic options.

In the early 1970s, Algeria nationalized—or took over from private owners—its oil industry. Algeria supported an embargo (ban) on the export of oil from Arab countries in 1973. The embargo caused the world price of oil to rise sharply. This brought a lot of money to Algeria. Boumediene used oil earnings to pay for industrial improvements, such as machinery. Little money went toward social services.

President Boumediene died in 1978. The FLN chose one of his aides, Chadli Bendjedid, as the new president. To improve Algeria's economy, Bendjedid cut back government ownership of Algerian industries and farms. However, corruption and bribery among government and military officials was high. Therefore, money mostly flowed into the hands of a few rich and powerful people.

To unify Algeria's people after generations of outside rule, the government tried to Arabize the nation. It emphasized its Arab heritage and removed French influences. Arabic became the official language of government and schools. Even street signs were changed to Arabic names, causing much confusion.

Many Berbers spoke French or the Berber language. A Berber cultural movement formed to oppose the forced Arabization. In April 1980, Berber college students went on strike to demand recognition of their culture. Government forces responded violently. Rioting led to thirty-two people's death. The government agreed to be more aware of the non-Arab minority. But tensions remained between Arabic-speaking and Berber-speaking Algerians.

The Rise of Islamists

During the 1980s, the gap between Algeria's rich and poor grew. Crime and corruption increased. Radical Islamist groups began to demand that Algeria adopt Sharia, or Islamic law. Islamists believed that the harsh but fair structure of Islam was the answer to Algeria's social problems. Their movement preached an ideal of a pure Islam free of Western influence, which many saw as immoral and materialistic.

Despite the ongoing unrest, Algerians reelected Bendjedid in 1984. In the mid-eighties, the world price of oil fell steeply. Algeria's economy suffered. Food, jobs, and housing became scarce. In October 1988, protesters took to the streets of Algiers. The army came in to control the unrest. Rioting throughout the country over the next ten days left 150 people dead.

The violence of "Black October" shocked the entire nation. Threatened with social breakdown, Bendjedid created a more democratic political system. Changes to the constitution made non-FLN political parties legal. Radical Islamist groups formed the Islamic Salvation Front (FIS) that year. Its goal was to make Algeria an Islamic state. While the political scene became livelier, the economy sank. Among youth, unemployment reached 50 percent. The FIS attracted many disillusioned young people.

More than fifty new parties ran in the first round of Algeria's 1991 elections. FIS won the majority of votes. The second round of elections was set for January 1992. It looked certain that FIS would win control of the legislature. The Islamists would be able to change Algeria's political system if they won. Rather than see this happen, the military canceled the elections. Military leaders forced President Bendjedid to resign. They established a five-member High State Council to run the country.

ISLAMISTS

Islam is a political and social system as well as a spiritual one. Sharia rules all aspects of society, from diet to crime. *Islamist* is a word used for people who believe Sharia should govern a country's private and public life. *Islamic fundamentalist* is a related term. Fundamentalists of any religion want strict obedience to the core values they believe in. Not all Muslims want a government based on Sharia. And not all Islamists support the use of force. However, extremist Islamist militants are willing to use violence for their cause of political Islam.

Debris lay in the street in Algiers after police and protesters clashed in October 1988. Security forces shot 25 people during the demonstration in the capital city. Rioting throughout the country left 150 people dead that month, called Black October.

The Algerian Civil War

Following the canceled elections, the High State Council declared a state of emergency. It shut down the legislature, outlawed the FIS, and arrested FIS followers.

Islamists' protests became violent. They targeted government offices and security forces (the police and soldiers). Using terror tactics such as car bombings, they killed foreigners, journalists, and politicians. Anyone who didn't support their movement was in danger.

By the end of 1992, Algeria found itself in a state of civil war. The Armed Islamic Group (GIA) emerged as the main rebel group pitted against the government's security forces. Once again, both sides engaged in terror, torture, and murder. The GIA pressured or even killed other Muslims who did not support them. They targeted women who did not cover themselves in traditional Islamic veils and robes. Pro-government death squads "disappeared" (illegally seized or murdered) thousands of civilians. FLN forces held suspects in desert concentration camps, as the French had once done to the FLN.

The High State Council chose General Liamine Zeroual as president in 1994. In 1996 the government outlawed all parties based on religion or ethnicity. A new Islamist group arose that year. The international Islamic network al-Qaeda helped form the Salafist Group for Preaching and Combat (GSPC).

By 1998 the government's security forces controlled most of the country. In early 1999, the military supported Abdelaziz Bouteflika in a rigged election, which he won. The new president concentrated on bringing stability to the war-torn country. In June 1999, the FIS agreed to end its fight. Bouteflika proposed an amnesty (legal pardon) for fighters. A nationwide vote approved the amnesty, which went into effect in 2000. The FIS laid down its arms. But hardcore members of the GIA, GSPC, and other small extremist groups kept fighting.

President Bouteflika announced that the civil war had claimed 150,000 lives. The cost to the country's infrastructure was $30 billion. Algerians call the 1990s the Black Decade.

Abdelaziz Bouteflika

The Twenty-First Century

The new millennium began with an improved economy and the hope of peace. Algeria's many challenges included severe shortages of jobs and housing. Almost 40 percent of the population lived on less than two dollars a day. Social services such as health care were poor. Bouteflika set up groups to improve schools and the legal system. But corruption limited solutions to the nation's problems. Meanwhile, small groups of Islamists continued to terrorize remote Algerian areas.

On September 11, 2001, al-Qaeda–aided terrorists attacked the United States. Following the attacks, the governments of Algeria and the United States worked together against global terrorism.

Berbers continued to demand greater rights in 2002. The legislature made the Berber language a national language. Arabic, however, remained the official language.

As Algeria continued to repair war damage, a powerful earthquake rocked the area east of Algiers in 2003. The quake killed at least 2,300 people and injured thousands more. Political violence that year included the Salafist Group's kidnapping of 32 European tourists. The German government paid millions of dollars in ransom money to the GSPC kidnappers.

Despite big challenges during his first term, Bouteflika reduced violence and brought some stability to Algeria. He encouraged investors from abroad to help develop the country's oil industry. Bouteflika has strong, personal control over the government. His rule limits full democratic development. Nonetheless, a number of political parties represent Algerians' interests. In the 2004 presidential elections, Louisa Hanoune became the first woman in Algeria's history to run for president. Voters, however, reelected Bouteflika in a landslide.

Officials arrested the head of the Armed Islamic Group in early 2005. This move ended the GIA, the main armed force still fighting the government. The government made progress with Berber leaders that year, allowing the use of Berber language in schools. With the end of the GIA, voters agreed to the president's plan for peace and reconciliation (forgiveness). This plan created a second amnesty. It does not forgive those involved in mass killings, rape, or bomb attacks in public places.

The amnesty became law in 2006. Toward the end of the year, however, al-Qaeda announced its support for the Algerian GSPC group. Al-Qaeda said the two groups would act together against French and U.S. interests. The expanding oil industry brings Algeria stability, but peace and full democracy in the nation remain elusive.

Government

The Algerian republic is based on a 1976 constitution, revised in 1989 and 1997. Since independence, Algeria's government has been in the hands of the FLN. Once the country's only legal political party, the FLN amended the Algerian constitution to allow opposition parties. The Ministry of Interior must approve all political parties. The constitution states that parties cannot be "based on differences in religion, language, race, gender, or region."

Algeria's citizens over the age of eighteen elect their president. The president serves five-year terms. The president appoints a cabinet (advisory group) of ministers and a prime minister. The prime minister oversees the cabinet and has the power to write laws. The twenty-six members of the cabinet supervise the various government departments, or ministries, such as education, environment, and health.

At presidential election time, jeeps carrying food, water, and ballot boxes travel to Algeria's remote regions. Officials set up hundreds of mobile voting stations so desert dwellers can vote.

Algeria's legislative branch consists of a bicameral (two-house) parliament, or legislature. Voters elect the 389 members of the lower house, the National People's Assembly. These members serve five-year terms. The senate, or upper house, has 144 seats. Voters elect two-thirds of its members to six-year terms. The president appoints the other third.

Algeria's legal system is based on French and Islamic law. The Supreme Court is the country's highest court. Lower courts meet in Algiers, Oran, and Constantine. There are forty-eight provincial courts. Local tribunals hear criminal and civil (noncriminal) cases. The death penalty exists only for people convicted of terrorist activities.

Algeria is divided into forty-eight provinces known as *wilayates*. The president appoints the provincial governors. There are also 691 communes—cities, towns, and villages. An elected assembly governs each province and commune. Municipal councils in Algeria's cities pass local laws, elect mayors, and appoint civil administrators.

THE PEOPLE

Algeria's population numbers 33 million people. The country's population density averages 36 people per square mile (14 people per sq. km). However, the population is not evenly spread out. More than 90 percent of the country's population lives on 12 percent of the country's land, along the Mediterranean coast. About 59 percent of Algeria's population lives in cities and towns. Settlement south of the Tell region is sparse.

Algeria has a high number of young people—31 percent are under the age of fifteen. Due to the large number of young women entering child-bearing age, Algeria's population will keep growing. Algerian women have an average of 2.4 children each. Experts estimate that Algeria's population will reach 41 million by 2025. The government views the birth rate as too high. It supports a national family planning program.

Years of civil strife and high unemployment have led many Algerians to leave the country. About 2 million Algerians live in France, where they often face discrimination.

Ethnic Groups

About 99 percent of Algerians are descended from Arabs and Berbers, reflecting centuries of intermarriage between the two groups. Europeans compose the remaining 1 percent of Algeria's population.

Arabs originally came from present-day Saudi Arabia. The Arab conquests of the seventh century brought Islam and the Arabic language to Algeria. The Arabs settled in cities and absorbed local customs. Meanwhile, the rural Berber peoples gradually adopted Islam. Their faith gives Arabs and Berbers a common identity as Muslims. Religion helped unify Arabs and Berbers during the war against the largely Roman Catholic colons.

Most Algerians identify with Arab language and culture. A minority of Algerians identify more with their Berber heritage. They call themselves Imazighen (Free People), as their ancestors did. Some of them work for greater recognition of Berber language and culture. A small movement for Berber independence wants self-rule for Berber regions.

This Tuareg family enjoys some hot tea. Tuareg people are part of the Berber group, a nomadic people that has lived in the region for centuries. Most Algerians are descended from Arabs and Berbers.

Berber traditions are strongest in the Kabylia region, southeast of Algiers. The Kabyle Berbers became an important class of merchants during French occupation. Originally from the Kabylia Mountains, the Kabyles established communities in other parts of the country. The Chaouia Berbers live in the Aurès Mountains near Constantine. The seven walled cities of the Mzab plateau in the northern Sahara are home to the Mzab Berber people. They have kept their separate culture within Algeria for more than one thousand years.

Farther south, nomadic Berber groups work as herders in the Sahara. The Tuareg people, a Berber group, live in southern Algeria as well as in Mali and Niger. Tuaregs travel across national borders in search of water, grazing land, and game. In recent decades, drought has dried up wells and killed many plants and animals. Therefore, many Tuaregs have settled in the scattered towns of southern Algeria.

After independence, most of the people of European descent living in Algeria left the country. During the civil war, Islamist extremists threatened to kill all westerners in Algeria. Of the 1 percent European population in modern Algeria, many are of French heritage.

Close to 200,000 Sahrawi refugees from Western Sahara also live in Algeria. They began arriving in the 1970s after a violent struggle broke out for control of their country. Morocco occupies Western Sahara, but the future of the land remains undecided. Most Sahrawi live in refugee camps in western Algeria's desert. They depend on international aid to survive.

Language

Algerians identify themselves by the language they speak more than their ethnic origins. More than 80 percent of Algerians speak Arabic. Close to 20 percent speak a dialect (variation) of the Berber language.

After independence, Arabic replaced French as the language of the government and schools as Algeria's official language. It is written from right to left in the Arabic alphabet. This Middle Eastern tongue spread through the region after the Arab conquest. Classical Arabic, the language of the Quran (the holy book of Islam), gradually became an international language of scholars, scientists, and writers throughout North Africa and the Middle East.

Algerians use two forms of modern Arabic—Modern Standard Arabic (MSA) and dialectical (conversational) Arabic. MSA is the language of the press and literature across the Arab world. It is also the spoken language of the media. Broadcasters on the all-Arab TV station Al Jazeera, for instance, speak MSA. Dialectical Arabic is the everyday language Algerians speak. Spoken across the Arab world, everyday

The **signs on this street** in El-Oued are written in Arabic and in the Roman alphabet. Arabic is the official language of Algeria, but the Berber language is also recognized. Some of the population still speak French as well.

Arabic varies widely among different nations. Over the centuries in Algeria, Arabic and Berber languages have exchanged many words.

The Algerians who speak a Berber dialect as their main language live mostly in rural regions. The Tuareg and Mzab peoples speak their own version of the Berber language. Some Berbers also use a distinctive alphabet.

French remains important as a language of business. Algerians in government often use French. Some newspapers are in French. Though it has no official status, French is still a second language for about 20 percent of Algerians.

PLAGUE IN ALGERIA

French Algerian author Albert Camus set *The Plague*—his most popular novel—in Oran. Camus describes how the citizens begin to notice rats dying. Soon the people begin to die horribly too. The plague had come to Oran. Rats don't cause plague, but they carry fleas that do. The bite of fleas infected with the bacteria *Yersinia pestis* spreads the disease. It starts with fever, chills, aches, and vomiting. In its most common form, bubonic plague, the bacteria invade lymph nodes. There the bacteria reproduce and cause buboes, or inflamed nodes. The painful buboes swell and break open. If untreated, plague kills 60 percent of its victims. Antibiotics cure the plague, if it is caught in time. Camus warned that the disease can lie dormant for years. *The Plague*'s final sentence states that at any time the plague could "rouse up its rats again and send them forth to die. . . ." In 2003 ten people in Oran got the plague. Nine survived. No new cases have been reported since then.

◉ Health

Algeria's government spends more than 4 percent of the national income on health, focusing on keeping its young population well. A major countrywide program of immunization (shots to prevent disease) has reduced childhood illnesses.

The government also supports education about pregnancy and child care. Health-care workers attend most births. The infant mortality rate—the IMR, or the number of babies who die within their first year of life—is 32 deaths per 1,000 births. This rate is better than the North African average IMR of 45 per 1,000. France's IMR is 4 per 1,000.

Algeria's average life expectancy is 73 years for males and 74 for females. Life ex-pectancy in North Africa as a whole is 68 years. France's life expectancy averages 80 years.

The government provides free health care to low-income

This Algerian woman's baby is treated at an international aid hospital.
People in rural areas of Algeria often do not have easy access to health care.

Algerians. Lines for care at clinics and hospitals are long. Therefore, people who can afford it often choose to pay for private doctors. The government requires doctors and dentists to work in public health for five years before they can go into private practice. This system improves Algerians' access to health care. Algeria has the low average of 1 physician per 1,000 people and 2 hospital beds per 1,000 people. Furthermore, most doctors work in the cities of the north. People in areas of low population often do not have easy access to medical care.

Overcrowding, poor sanitation, unclean water, and a lack of nutritious food—especially in rural areas—cause many of Algeria's health problems. The leading diseases are tuberculosis (a lung disease), hepatitis, measles, typhoid fever, cholera, and dysentery. Trachoma, an eye disease, is also a serious problem,

HUMAN DEVELOPMENT INDEX

One way of looking at the welfare of a nation's people is to consult the United Nations' Human Development Index. It ranks 177 countries by comparing key areas such as health, schooling, and income. Lower numbers reflect higher development. Algeria ranks 108 out of 177, better than Morocco (125) but behind Tunisia (92) and Libya (58). France ranks 16, and the United States ranks 8. For links to websites on the Human Development Index, visit www.vgsbooks.com.

especially in poor or rural areas. Easily spread from person to person, trachoma is a leading cause of blindness.

About 0.1 percent of Algeria's adult population is living with HIV/AIDS (human immunodeficiency virus/acquired immunodeficiency syndrome). HIV spreads through body fluids, usually through sexual intercourse or sharing intravenous needles. Medicines help people with HIV/AIDS survive, but the drugs are very expensive.

Education

In 1976 the government began a complete reform of the educational system. It replaced the country's private, French-language schools with public schools. Arabic became the language of school instruction. In 2003 the government allowed Berber-language instruction.

Algerians value education, and the government spends almost 20 percent of its budget to provide free schooling. By law, children between the ages of six and fifteen are required to attend school. Attendance is high in cities but drops in rural areas. Only 50 percent of children continue on to high school. Many need to work to help support their families.

Despite improvements since independence, fewer girls than boys attend school. Algeria's literacy rate reflects this difference. About 94 percent of young men fifteen to twenty-four years old are able to read

These students are ready to begin studying on the first day of school.

Huts made of grasses in a Tuareg village and a **mud brick house** are just two of the different kinds of shelters Algerians live in. The type of house people live in largely depends on whether they are in the cities on the coast or living in villages in the mountains or desert.

and write. But only 86 percent of young women the same age are literate. Literacy rates for Algerians overall are 77 percent for males and 59 percent for females.

Algeria has ten universities. The University of Algiers is the largest. Opened in 1879, this institution enrolls more than 100,000 students. It has separate schools of law, medicine, science, Islamic studies, and the liberal arts. The nation also has several technical colleges. The Algerian government emphasizes teacher training and technical and scientific courses of study. It also funds adult literacy programs.

Ways of Life

Algerians lead a wide variety of lifestyles. But for most, the family is of central importance. Family loyalty and honor are important to Algerians. Family members expect to give and to get emotional and economic support from one another. Marriages are seen as the union of two families, not just two individuals. Sometimes parents arrange marriages, but many young people choose their own marriage partners.

Algerians' lifestyles depend partly on where they live. In the countryside, most

Many Algerian men wear a mustache as a symbol of manliness. To curse a man's mustache is a very rude insult in Algeria.

Algerian women may dress in Western-style clothing or in traditional clothing, such as a haik. How a woman dresses may depend on where she lives. Men's hooded cloaks are called burnooses.

people work as farmers or herders. Some work on oil rigs. Extended families, including grandparents, often live together. Wood is scarce, so houses are made of sun-dried mud bricks. Nomads shelter in tents. Traditional clothing is common in rural areas. Women wear blouses and skirts. In public they may wear a sheetlike garment called a haik. Men wear long, flowing robes or shirts and loose-fitting trousers. They may also wear a burnoose—a one-piece cloak with a hood. Drought, poverty, and political violence in rural Algeria have forced many people to move to the cities.

In urban areas, Algerians work in factories, government jobs, businesses, and many other occupations. European culture and clothing such as jeans are more common in cities than in the countryside. Average families live in crowded apartment buildings or concrete houses. Usually only parents and children live together. Because of a scarcity of work and housing in cities, young Algerians are putting off getting married. The average age at which urban Algerians marry has increased to thirty for women and thirty-three for men.

Women

Algeria is a patriarchal society. That is, men hold more social and political power than women. Women played a crucial role in the Algerian Revolution. Many Algerians hoped that independence would bring social and political equality for women. Under pressure from Islamists, however, the government adopted Algeria's 1984 Family Code. This set of laws gives women the same legal status as children in many areas of life. Men have the legal right to decide whether or not their wives hold jobs, for instance.

Algerian women have the right to vote, and women make up 6 percent of the legislature. Defenders of woman's rights work to repeal (remove) the Family Code, but it remains in place.

The way women dress has significance in Algeria. Islam teaches that women should dress modestly. Algerian Muslims interpret this in different ways at different times. Over the centuries, many women followed the Arab tradition of wearing robes and face veils in public. The French government encouraged Western clothing. During the Algerian Revolution, some women turned to traditional clothing to show their pride in being Muslim and their resistance to French rule. After independence, urban women often dressed in Western fashions. During the civil war of the 1990s, Islamists pressured women to cover themselves in robes and veils again. Extremists even killed some women who refused. In modern big cities, about half the women wear traditional clothes, either to respect tradition or to avoid being harassed by Islamists.

Berber women are generally less restricted than Arab women. Unlike Arab women, Berber women do not veil their faces. Among the Tuareg, it is the men who veil their faces. The origin of this tradition is unknown, but it is probably related to the need for protection from sun and wind, not modesty.

CULTURAL LIFE

Algeria has been a gateway between Africa, Europe, and the Middle East since ancient times. Berbers adopted parts of many cultures, while keeping their own unique traditions. Arab culture had the most lasting effects on modern Algeria, especially through the Arabic language and Islamic religion. However, other cultures left their imprints all over the country, from Roman ruins to French-language newspapers.

▷ Religion

Islam is Algeria's state religion and the faith of 99 percent of the population. The remaining 1 percent of Algerians are Christians. Most Christians practice Roman Catholicism, a religion introduced by the French. Algeria's once large Jewish population mostly identified with France and left the country after independence. Most moved to France or Israel.

Islam is a monotheistic (one-god) religion that shares roots with Judaism and Christianity. Muslims believe that the angel Gabriel

revealed God's final messages to the prophet Muhammad in the seventh century. These words are recorded in Islam's holy book, the Quran. Muslims traditionally look to Islam for political guidance as well as for spiritual inspiration. They consult both the Quran and the *hadith*, the written collection of Muhammad's sayings and deeds. These sources are the basis of Islamic law.

Like Christianity, Islam has many branches. Most Algerians follow Sunni Islam—the majority branch. Sunni Islam traces its leadership back to the first elected leaders after Muhammad. (The other main branch, Shia, traces its leadership to Muhammad's relatives.) The Sufi branch of Islam also has followers in Algeria. Sufism is a mystical approach to Islam. Mysticism encourages personal practices to bring an individual closer to God. Berber Muslim groups may also include elements of folk religion in their beliefs. These include honoring holy figures of Islam as saints. This practice goes against strict Islamic tradition, which considers all Muslims equal.

Devout Muslims of all branches strive to fulfill Islam's five basic duties. These are known as the five pillars of Islam. The duties are making a statement of faith in Allah and his prophet Muhammad; praying five times daily; fasting during the holy month of Ramadan; giving to charity; and making a pilgrimage to the holy city of Mecca, Saudi Arabia, if possible.

Algeria's government allows non-Muslims to practice their religions. However, laws limit religious freedom. For instance, it is illegal to try to convert Muslims to other religions. The government financially supports Algeria's mosques and pays for the training of imams (Muslim clergy). Islam is taught in public schools. However, the government also outlaws any Muslim teaching or preaching that calls for violence.

Holidays

Islamic holy days follow a lunar (moon-based) calendar. The years are counted from Muhammad's journey from Mecca to Medina, Saudi Arabia, in 622. Muslims celebrate this journey, called the hegira, on Muharram 1, the first day of the Muslim year. Friday is the holy day of the week for Muslims. Men go to the mosque to hear teachings and

The engraving on the **minaret, or tower,** on this mosque in Tlemcen shows the way Muslim artists have used geometric design in mosques. In Algeria, mosques are built to resemble the house of the prophet Muhammad where the first Muslims met. Four walls surround a central courtyard. A hall for prayer stands on one side of the mosque. Often a large dome covers the mosque's central hall. A tall minaret rises from one corner. From the minaret, a muezzin, or crier, calls the faithful to prayer. In modern times, the call to prayer is often a recording.

to pray. Women pray at home or in separate parts of the mosque.

The most important Islamic holy time is the month of Ramadan. This is the month when Muhammad became Allah's prophet. Observant Muslims do not drink or eat anything between sunrise and sunset all month. The whole country slows down during the day. However, shops and cafés open at night. Ramadan ends with two days of feasts and worship, called Eid al-Fitr. The other main Islamic holidays are Mouloud (Muhammad's birthday) and Eid al-Kebir, or the Feast of the Sacrifice. On this feast, people who can afford it have a sheep slaughtered and share the meat with the poor.

Algeria celebrates its 1962 independence from France on July 5. Other secular (nonreligious) holidays include New Year's Day (January 1), Labor Day (May 1), Ben Bella's Overthrow (June 19), and the Anniversary of the Revolution (November 1).

The Arts

Love of abstract pattern and color is a hallmark of Islamic art. Islam discourages drawings of people and animals in religious art. Therefore, Muslim artists mastered geometric design. Floral and mathematical formulas are the basis for many designs. Calligraphy (decorative handwriting) is an art form in itself, traditionally used in elegantly handwritten Qurans. Designs and beautifully written verses appear on Algerian mosques, civic buildings, and craftwork such as carpets and pottery.

In the twentieth century, Algeria gradually developed new artistic styles. Many Algerian artists draw on ancient Islamic motifs in their works. Painter Mohamed Racim (1896–1975) brought modern colors to traditional miniature paintings. Modern Algerians explore abstract painting or paint about social concerns, such as war. M'Hamed Issiakhem (1928–1985) was a pioneer of modern Algerian painting. In works such as *Homage to Katia*, Issiakhem's female figures especially express emotion and suffering.

Algeria also has a thriving tradition of crafts. Skilled craftspeople create carpets, ceramics, leatherwork, silverwork, pottery, and musical instruments. Handmade Algerian goods are sold in many other countries, as well as to tourists.

Literature

Algeria has a rich and long tradition of literature. For thousands of years, people have passed on tales and beliefs through word of mouth. Kabyle Berbers are the source of much oral folklore in modern Algeria. Music and dance sometimes go along with the storytelling.

During Roman times, the Algerian Berber writer Apuleius of Madauros (ca. A.D. 123–180) wrote Africa's first novel. This funny

ALGERIAN PROVERBS

Traditional sayings called proverbs display a culture's wisdom and point of view. Following are a few of Algeria's many proverbs:

• A reasonable enemy is better than a narrow-minded friend.

• Patience is the key to paradise.

• Speak kindly or don't speak.

• Peace wins over wealth.

• The hand that gives is better than the hand that receives.

• A friend shares both your joy and your pain.

• When I think of someone else's problems, I forget mine.

• A secret between two people is soon nobody's secret.

novel, *The Golden Ass*, tells the tale of unlucky Lucius, who accidentally turns into a long-eared ass. Saint Augustine (354–430), born near modern Constantine, emerged as an important writer toward the end of the Roman era. A leader of the early Christian church, Augustine wrote of his spiritual search in his autobiography, the *Confessions*.

In the centuries after the Arab conquest, many Islamic scholars, poets, and historians in Algeria wrote in Arabic. Most famous for his resistance against the French, Abd al-Qadir (1807–1883) was also an author. He wrote about religion, science, and military affairs. Algeria also attracted foreign writers over the years. European writer Isabella Eberhardt (1877–1904) explored North Africa, dressed as a man. She married an Algerian and converted to Islam. A collection of her writings is available in English as *The Oblivion Seekers*.

During the French occupation, many Algerian authors wrote in French. Albert Camus (1913–1960) was an Algerian writer of French ancestry. He won the Nobel Prize in Literature in 1957. Many of Camus's essays and novels describe his existentialist or absurdist philosophy—the idea that life holds no ultimate meaning, such as religion offers. His heroes in novels such as *The Plague* (1947) often face hopeless situations. However, they find meaning in dignity, kindness, and bravery.

Albert Camus

Kateb Yacine (1929–1989) and Mohammed Dib (1920–2003) were part of a group of writers known as the Generation of 1954. This generation witnessed the Algerian Revolution. Liberation and the search for identity are major themes in their writings. Kateb Yacine's most famous novel, *Nedjma* (1956), weaves together memories of his childhood, love for his cousin Nedjma, and Algerian history. A freethinker, he said of himself that he was not Arab or Muslim but Algerian. Dib's novels focus on the changes war and modernization brought to rural Algerians.

Tahar Djaout (1954–1993) was a novelist, poet, and journalist whose writings offended Islamist groups. Djaout's final novel, *The Last Summer of Reason*, was published after his murder at the hands of extremists. It is a horrifying fantasy about a fundamentalist group taking over society.

Critics consider Assia Djebar (b. 1936) one of the leading writers in North Africa. Her work brings the private side of Algeria to light and uses it to talk about far-reaching issues. She often describes the cost of war and oppression on Algeria's women. *Women of Algiers in Their Apartment* is a collection of her short stories. Djebar also makes films.

"SPEAK OUT AND DIE"

During Algeria's civil war, extremists assassinated writers and other people who spoke out against them. And both sides slaughtered thousands of ordinary citizens caught in the middle, who only wanted to live in peace. Writer Tahar Djaout expressed the frustration of this no-win situation. He called for bravery in the face of death in his short-lived newspaper *Ruptures*. Extremists killed Djaout in 1993. But these lines he wrote remain famous in Algeria:

"Silence is death
And you, if you speak, you die,
If you remain silent, you die,
So speak out and die."

—Quoted in Julija Sukys, *Silence Is Death: The Life and Work of Tahar Djaout* (Lincoln and London: University of Nebraska Press, 2007), 118–119.

Film and Media

Many Algerian filmmakers have made films about the reality of life in their country. After independence, the government hired a filmmaker to portray the Algerian war against France. The result was Italian director Gillo Pontecorvo's world-famous film, *Battle of Algiers* (1966). Pontecorvo filmed in Algiers's casbah and employed locals as actors. The film has gained new audiences in the current era of global terrorism.

Award-winning director Mohamed Lakhdar-Hamina is a pioneer of Algerian cinema. His 1967 film, *The Wind of the Aurès Mountains*, tells the tale of a Berber woman who loses both her husband and her son in the war of independence. The director's son Malik Lakhdar-Hamina is a filmmaker too. Director Kamal Dehane makes documentary films. For his 1998 film *Algeria, The Children Speak*, Dehane interviewed children growing up during Algeria's civil war. He mixed the interviews with

Algeria has caught the imagination of many foreign filmmakers. Algiers's casbah received the Hollywood treatment in the 1938 romance *Algiers*. The story about a jewel thief was a U.S. remake of the 1937 French film *Pepe Le Moko*. The award-winning French thriller *Caché* (*Hidden*, 2005) explores France's murky relationship with its Algerian past.

images of children living forty years earlier to show that little had changed.

Algeria's government tightly controls the mass media, including television and radio stations. It is illegal to defame (insult) the government or the army in the media. Algerian courts have sent dozens of journalists to prison. Being a reporter has sometimes even been deadly in Algeria. During the 1990s, Islamist extremist groups murdered fifty-seven journalists. Nonetheless, Algeria's private press can be very outspoken. Some privately owned newspapers hold a yearly "day without newspapers" to protest the defamation laws. On Independence Day 2006, President Bouteflika pardoned all convicted journalists. But the laws that restrict free expression remain in place.

Music

A wealth of styles represents Algerian music. Refugees from Spain after 1492 brought Andalus music to North Africa. This classical music reflects the meeting of Jewish, Christian, and Muslim cultures in Spain. Berber music is traditionally performed with flutes, bagpipes, drums, and tambourines. After the 1980 rise of Berber culture, Kabyle artists became better known on the national level. Singer Lounes Matoub expressed the Berbers' longing for an independent homeland. Extremists assassinated him in 1998. Traditional Bedouin music also survives in rural areas. Bedouin musicians chant long stories to the sound of flutes and drums.

Raï is Algeria's most popular modern style at home and abroad. It fuses centuries-old folk music with pop, rock, and rap. Raï musicians use drums, mandolins, and rosewood flutes blended with synthesizers and modern instruments. They sing of the pain and pleasure of love in what some people call the blues of Algeria. They also express political opinions, especially frustration with both the government and fundamentalism. Cheikha (a title meaning "elder") Remitti (1923–2006) is known as the Queen of Raï. Khaled is known as the King of Raï. His 2004 album *Ya-Rahi* (Oh My!) is subtitled *Love to the People—Peace through Music*. Cheb i Sabbah released *La Kahena* in 2005. The album's title refers to the legendary Berber queen. Sabbah collaborated with several North African women singers on this album. It reached number six

These young Algerian women play traditional music. Music in Algeria takes many different forms from the many cultures that influenced the country.

on *Billboard* magazine's world charts. Due to Algeria's limited freedom of expression, many Algerian musicians live in France.

Sports and Recreation

Many young Algerian men are enthusiastic participants in sports. Algerian girls and women play sports too but less so than males. Soccer (called football in Algeria) is the country's most popular sport. The Algerian national soccer team, the Desert Foxes, competes internationally.

Algerians also enjoy basketball, handball, and volleyball. The country's sports facilities include swimming pools, tennis courts, and ski resorts. Along the Mediterranean Sea, resorts offer waterskiing, sailing, and other ocean sports. Both Algerians and tourists enjoy horseback riding, mountain hiking, and camping. In the desert regions, horse racing and camel racing are old pastimes. The "fantasia" is a display of horse-riding skills. It includes mock battle charges, in which horses gallop while their riders shoot at targets.

Algerian athletes excel at running. Algerians competed for France in the Olympic Games during the years Algeria was part of France.

Visit www.vgsbooks.com for links to websites with additional information about the sports and recreational activities Algerians enjoy.

These **Berber youngsters play soccer** in the region of Algeria near the Aurès Mountains. Soccer is the most popular sport for Algerian children to play. Soccer star Zinedine Zidane is a national hero in Algeria. He grew up in France with his Algerian parents. Algerians cheered for Zidane and the French soccer team in the 2006 World Cup. In the last game of the tournament, Zidane head-butted (slammed his head into) an Italian player who insulted him. Officials "red-carded" Zidane (banned him from play). Italy won the World Cup.

Algerian runner Alain Mimoun won a gold medal for France in the 1956 Olympics. In 1992 Hassiba Boulmerka became the first Olympic gold medalist for Algeria's own team. She won the 1,500-meter race. Nouria Merah-Benida won Algeria's only gold medal at the 2000 Olympics, also for the women's 1,500-meter race.

Algerians love to socialize with family and friends, and they highly value hospitality. Women and men normally spend leisure time separately, except for family outings, such as picnics and trips to the beach. Women usually gather in homes. Men often socialize in cafés, where they play chess and other games.

Food

Algerian cooking blends flavors and recipes from many sources, including the Middle East and France. Algerians often shop daily at outdoor markets or supermarkets. The scents and colors of mint, lemon, and rose petals used in cooking delight the senses. Local vegetables include tomatoes, eggplants, green beans, potatoes, and onions. Mediterranean groves provide a bounty of olives, figs, and almonds. Seafood includes shrimp, bass, perch, and anchovies.

A North African dish known as couscous is popular all over Algeria. Cooks steam couscous (tiny grains of pasta) and serve it with a spicy stew. Cinnamon, cloves, and sometimes raisins add sweetness. The stew may contain chicken, beef, or mutton (the meat of sheep). Devout Muslims do not eat pork, by religious law.

Main courses often include mutton and lamb, sometimes grilled on a spit. Cooking meat with fruits and nuts is a common feature of Algerian dishes. Chicken with almonds and lamb with apricots are favorites. Various soups are also popular. *Chorba beida* is chicken soup with vegetables, pasta, and egg yolk. *Tajine* is the name both of a stew

ALGERIAN VEGETABLE COUSCOUS

The stew that goes on top of couscous appears in many forms. This is a vegetarian version of Algeria's national dish. Feel free to substitute other vegetables and adjust the spices. If you like, add ½ cup raisins to the stew when you add the garbanzo beans.

1 onion, chopped	1 turnip, peeled
2 tbsp. olive oil	2 zucchini
½ tsp. turmeric	2 yellow summer squash
½ tsp. cayenne	4 carrots, peeled
½ tsp. black pepper	4 potatoes, peeled
⅛ tsp. cinnamon	1 bell pepper, seeded
2 whole cloves	1 15 oz. can garbanzo beans
1 tsp. salt	1 c. couscous
1 6 oz. can tomato paste	1½ c. boiling water
½ c. water	

1. In a large pan, fry onion in olive oil over medium heat until translucent (clear).
2. Add spices, salt, tomato paste, and ½ c. water to onions. Mix, and cook for 5 more minutes.
3. Cut the vegetables in large chunks. Add to onion mix, and cover with cold water. Bring to a boil, then turn heat to low. Cover pan, and simmer for 15 minutes.
4. Drain and rinse the garbanzo beans. Add to vegetables, and cook for 15 more minutes.
5. Pour boiling water over couscous in a bowl, and cover. Wait about 5 minutes. Fluff with fork.
6. Serve the vegetable stew over the couscous.

Serves 4 to 6.

and the clay pot it is cooked in. *Harissa*, a seasoning of red pepper, salt, and garlic, adds heat to many recipes. Rice often accompanies these flavorful dishes. Baking crusty loaves of bread is a French tradition. Arab flatbreads are common too.

Baklava is a dessert of chopped nuts, honey, and sugar layered in thin sheets of pastry. Fruits such as oranges or dates are almost always offered for dessert. Diners enjoy sweet mint tea or coffee after meals. Algerian wines have a good international reputation. Muslims who follow Islamic law do not drink alcohol.

THE ECONOMY

Following independence in 1962, the FLN government ran Algeria along Socialist lines. The state tightly controlled the economy. It took ownership of most foreign-owned businesses. In the late 1980s, high unemployment and food shortages caused strikes and violent protests. In response, the government created a more open system, allowing private ownership. For most of the 1990s, however, economic troubles and civil war racked the country.

In the twenty-first century, peace and high earnings from oil and natural gas have caused Algeria's economy to grow steadily. But high unemployment and a low standard of living continue to be major challenges for the government. The unemployment rate is 30 percent overall. It climbs to 50 percent among Algerians under thirty years old. The government is increasing spending to create and pay for jobs and to improve living standards. It employs many workers to build housing, roads, and water systems.

Algeria is a low- to middle-income country. Its average income per

person is about $6,000 per year. This is a little higher than average for countries developing their industries and for North Africa. Countries with developed industries, such as France, average $26,000 per person.

Algeria's wealth is not evenly shared among its people. About 25 percent of the Algerian population lives below the poverty line (less than $2 per day). The top 10 percent of the population holds about 45 percent of Algeria's wealth. This situation is partly a reflection of corruption among public officials, business owners, and military officials. Bribery and illegal deals drain profits into the pockets of a few powerful people. A black market (illegal trade in goods) also thrives in Algeria.

Algeria's economy is also not well balanced. Its oil and gas industry accounts for about 30 percent of the country's total earnings. Because the world price of oil is not stable, Algeria does not want to depend on it for such a large part of its income. In order to diversify the economy, the government encourages the growth of other industries.

Industry

In the 1990s, the government privatized (opened to private investors) Algeria's industry. Local and foreign investors were welcomed. However, civil war reduced industrial growth and scared off investors. Islamist extremists damaged factories and other industries in an attempt to weaken the state. The reduction of violence in the late 1990s and a series of reforms led to industrial growth.

Industry provides 53 percent of the gross domestic product (GDP, or the value of goods and services a country produces yearly). The industrial sector employs 23 percent of the workforce. It includes jobs in manufacturing, construction, and mining. The production and refining of hydrocarbons (oil and natural gas) dominates the industrial sector.

Algerian quarries produce fine onyx and marble. Sculptors and architects have appreciated these beautiful minerals since Roman times. The stones are hard enough to carve into fine detail and can be polished until they shine.

Manufacturing includes heavy industries, such as oil refining, steelmaking, and chemical production. Nearly all of Algeria's heavy industries are located on or near the Mediterranean coast. Seawater desalination plants provide much-needed water. Factories produce iron, concrete, and other building materials for new apartments and other building projects.

Smaller firms make furniture, plastic goods, textiles, leather, and clothing. Food-processing companies produce olive oil and Algerian wine. Some factories process tobacco. Much of the food is exported to France and other European countries.

Algeria also has extensive reserves of iron ore, the raw material for finished iron and steel products. In addition, companies extract phosphates from mines near Algeria's border with Tunisia. Factories use phosphates to make agricultural fertilizer. Other important mineral resources include coal, lead, zinc, mercury, salt, and uranium. Small mines produce gold and semiprecious stones.

Hydrocarbons and Energy

Oil was discovered in the eastern Sahara in 1956. French-owned companies built a network of wells, refineries, and pipelines in Algeria. In 1971 the FLN government took ownership of the country's oil industry. The state-owned company Sonatrach has controlled Algeria's oil production, refining, and transporting since then. Income from the sale of energy products abroad helped Algeria develop other sectors of the economy. In 2005 the legislature passed a series of laws opening up the oil industry to private investors. The government hopes to double the number of oil companies in Algeria by inviting more foreign investors. Algeria continues to invest in exploration and has found new oil and gas reserves.

Algeria's largest oil field is Hassi Messaoud, in the center of the country. It holds about 60 percent of the country's oil. Pipelines transfer hydrocarbons from oil fields to the coast. Large refineries near the Mediterranean coast process petroleum (crude oil) and natural gas. Seven terminals on the coast export petroleum, refined oil, and natural gas.

Natural gas occurs alongside petroleum, and Algeria has one of the largest gas reserves in the world. Companies continue to explore and develop the industry. The government dominates the gas industry but is opening the sector to private gas producers.

Algeria uses 26 percent of its natural gas for its own energy needs. Gas meets 64 percent of the country's energy needs, including 99 percent of its electricity. Hydropower, or the power of rushing water, supplies less than 1 percent of Algeria's electricity. Petroleum supplies the rest of Algeria's energy. The country exports the remaining 74 percent of its natural gas to Europe and the United States.

The **oil refinery** at Hassi Messaoud, Algeria's largest oil field, transfers oil from the field to pipelines that take the oil to the coast. Algeria is also the biggest supplier of natural gas to Europe. Two plastic, underwater pipelines carry natural gas between the continents. The Trans-Mediterranean pipeline from Algeria to Italy extends 670 miles (1,078 km). The Maghreb-Europe Gas pipeline to Spain is 1,000 miles (1,609 km) long.

Services and Tourism

Service occupations provide business, private, and public services rather than producing goods. Algeria's service sector accounts for 37 percent of Algeria's GDP. It employs 63 percent of the workforce. It includes jobs in government, health care, education, banking, retail trade, and tourism.

Algeria's government is by far the largest service employer. It spends a large amount of its budget hiring medical workers, teachers, laborers, administrators, and more.

Algeria was once a major tourist destination. In the 1980s, the government built new hotels and resorts to take advantage of Algeria's sunny climate and ocean beaches. Many tourists visited Algeria's historic sites. These range from Algiers's casbah to the prehistoric rock art of Tassili N'Ajjer. Algeria's tourist industry almost totally disappeared in the 1990s, however, due to the civil war. By 2000 the security situation had improved. That year 866,000 tourists brought $102 million to the country. (In comparison, neighboring Morocco earns $2 billion yearly in tourism.) However, the kidnapping of European tourists in 2003 illustrates the ongoing danger of travel in Algeria.

Agriculture, Fishing, and Forestry

Agriculture, including forestry and fishing, provides 10 percent of Algeria's GDP. The sector employs 14 percent of the labor force. Most of Algeria's land is not suitable for farming. Therefore, food scarcity has long been a challenge for Algeria, and the nation must import food.

The state took ownership of many of Algeria's large farms during the 1960s. After years of state ownership, in the 1980s, the government allowed many farmers to buy the land they worked.

Most of Algeria's farmland lies on or near the Mediterranean coastline. Wheat, barley, and oats are the main grain crops. Serious droughts since the 1990s have reduced harvests, and Algeria imports much grain from Canada, France, and the United States. Also suited to the warm, dry climate of the Tell region are citrus fruits, vegetables, wine grapes, olive trees, and fig trees.

DESALINATION

Desalination is the process of creating drinkable water from salt water. In huge factories, seawater is heated so steam rises, leaving the heavier salt behind. The steam collects, cools, and condenses back into water in huge vats. This process repeats over and over until the water is free of salt.

Two women watch children playing in the Mediterranean Sea on a popular beach near Algiers. Visit www.vgsbooks.com for links to websites with other fun activities children in Algeria enjoy.

In the oases of the Sahara, farmers grow grains and vegetables on small plots. Plantations of date palms are common near desert water sources. Algeria is one of the world's leading exporters of dates.

Herders raise sheep and goats in the north, as well as in the lower elevations of the Saharan Atlas. Farmers also raise cattle for dairy production and camels and donkeys as work animals. Drought and disease limit the size of Algeria's herds and keep meat and milk production low.

Algeria's fishers harvest the Mediterranean Sea. Most fishing boats are small, family-owned craft. Tuna, sardines, bluefish, anchovies, and shellfish are sold on the domestic market. Spain, France, and Italy are the major export markets.

Centuries of unrestricted logging have reduced forested areas to less than 1 percent of Algeria's total land area. Loggers cut down Algeria's pine, cedar, and oak trees for building materials. Rural people harvest trees for fuel. Sawn timber supplies the construction industry, and Algerian farmers strip cork from cork oak trees. The leather industry uses bark for tanning (processing hides). The government oversees reforestation (tree replacement) and conservation efforts.

Transportation and Communication

Algeria's colon administrators built an extensive road network in the country's north before the war for independence. In 2005 Algeria's government awarded contracts to companies to build six-lane roads crisscrossing the country.

About 64,622 miles (104,000 km) of roads connect Algeria's cities, towns, and ports. Of these roads, 44,525 miles (71,656 km) are paved. The paved Trans-Saharan Highway runs north and south. It is a main route for tourists and for trucks that carry goods between the nations of northern and western Africa. Passenger cars number about 2.5 per 100 people. Algeria's road and rail networks do not reach isolated oases. Camels, four-wheel-drive vehicles, or airplanes are the best form of transportation in some remote desert regions.

A railroad system runs from the Mediterranean Sea southward and also links Mediterranean ports and remote oil fields. Buses serve many of the country's smaller towns and villages.

Air Algérie, the national airline, flies domestic and international routes. The country has 137 airports, 52 of which have paved runways. The main international airport is at Algiers. Other airports provide an important link to the towns and oases of the south, which are difficult to reach over land. The busy ports handle Algeria's industrial and oil exports, as well as travelers.

DONKEY SMUGGLERS

In 2003 officials captured two hundred donkeys working in the black market. Smugglers had found a way to sneak illegal goods back and forth across the border of Algeria and Morocco. They loaded the goods on donkeys and attached tape recorders to their backs. As the trained donkeys followed a rural track, the recorded message on their backs repeated the word *err*, which means "walk" in Arabic. Once across the border, the donkeys were met by smugglers who unloaded their burdens. The smugglers rewound the tapes, reloaded the donkeys with different goods, and sent them back again.

Algeria's telephone system is outdated and inefficient, especially in the south. Only about 2.3 million landlines are in use. However, Algerians use almost 5 million cellular phones. Internet users number about 1 million. Cybercafes offer Algerians access to computers and the Internet for a fee.

Trade

In 2001 Algeria reached an agreement with the European Union (EU, an organization that removes legal barriers to the movement of goods and people in Europe). In order to expand trade between them, Algeria and the EU both cut tariffs (taxes on imports).

Huge oil and natural gas reserves supply more than 96 percent of Algeria's exports. The country is a member of the Organization of Petroleum Exporting Countries (OPEC).

Other important Algerian

exports include citrus fruits, iron ore, phosphates, tobacco, cork, and wine. The country's major export partners are the United States, Italy, France, and Spain. Algeria's main imports are machinery, raw materials, food, iron, steel, and textiles. France is Algeria's main import partner. Since the nineteenth century, France has been the biggest buyer of Algerian wine. French companies also invest in Algerian businesses and industries. Italy, Germany, and Spain are also important import partners for Algeria.

The Future

The government's most pressing economic challenge is to diversify the economy. The government works to attract foreign companies to invest in Algeria toward this goal.

Though the FLN government has kept control of the country, Algeria's political future is somewhat uncertain. Some Algerians seek to reshape society according to strict Islamic law. Other Algerians fear the sweeping changes that could occur if Islamists control the government. Politicians debate whether or not to allow extreme Islamist parties to run in democratic elections. President Bouteflika's strong control of the government also limits the full development of democracy.

The country continues to struggle with many long-standing social problems. Despite improvements, wide social gaps exist between rich and poor Algerians. Legal and social discrimination against women also persists. The government aims to make further education and health-care reforms. It also works to provide reliable water and electricity throughout the country. But as long as many Algerians do not have jobs and adequate housing, the nation's peace does not rest on stable ground.

MILLENNIUM DEVELOPMENT GOALS

In 2000, at the dawn of the millennium, leaders of 191 countries—including Algeria—agreed on a plan. It was a vision of a world with less poverty, hunger, and disease. They created the Millennium Development Goals (MDG) to work toward cutting extreme global poverty in half by 2015. Leaders agreed to work for equal opportunities for women and lower death rates for children. Other challenges include combating disease, providing clean water, and protecting the environment. The countries also pledged to partner with other countries to help achieve the MDG worldwide. The challenges are great, but Algeria is struggling to create a better future. By 2007 Algeria had made its largest strides in education and health. The empowerment of women made slow progress. Environmental statistics remained about the same.

CA. 8000 B.C.   Artists illustrate the ways of life on rock walls in southeast Algeria during the Sahara's wet period.

CA. 4000 B.C.   Climate change begins to turn the Sahara to desert.

CA. 1200 B.C.   Phoenician traders establish trading posts along Algeria's coast.

CA. 200 B.C.   Masinissa, the Berber leader of Numidia, establishes his capital at Cirta (modern Constantine).

146 B.C.   Rome defeats the Carthaginian Empire and begins to settle the North African coast.

A.D. 429   The Vandals invade North Africa, including Algeria.

CA. 500   Byzantine forces defeat the Vandals and rule Algeria's coast.

632   The prophet Muhammad dies. Afterward, Arab Muslim armies set out to conquer North Africa, including Algeria. They call the region the Maghreb.

700S   The Arab Abbasid dynasty gains control of North Africa.

LATE 800S   Berbers from the Kabylia region install the Arab Fatimid dynasty.

LATE 900S   Fatimid control weakens as Berber chieftains rise in power.

1056   The Almoravids rule North Africa, including many Algerian cities.

MID-1100S   The Almohads replace the Almoravids as rulers of the Maghreb.

1492   Many Muslims and Jews forced out of Spain move to Algeria. Spain seizes some of Algeria's ports.

1518   Muslim leader Khayr al-Din (Barbarossa) gains control of Algiers. North Africa's Barbary Coast gradually becomes a safe haven for pirates.

1546   The Ottoman Turks take control of al-Din's realm.

1671   The pirate guild replaces the Ottoman representative in Algiers with a governor called a dey.

1815   U.S. ships enter the harbor of Algiers to force an end to piracy.

1830   France invades and conquers northern Algeria.

1847   The French defeat powerful Muslim rebel leader Abd al-Qadir and gain control of Algeria.

1914   Algerian troops fight with the French against Germany in World War I (1914–1918). Veterans of the war begin to organize for independence after the war.

1942 Allied forces land in Algeria to drive German and Italian forces from North Africa during World War II (1939-1945).

1954 The FLN launches the Algerian Revolution against French rule on November 1.

1956 Oil is discovered in eastern Algeria's desert.

1957 Algerian writer Albert Camus wins the Nobel Prize in Literature.

1962 Algeria becomes independent on July 3. FLN founder Ahmed Ben Bella is the country's first president.

1965 Army commander Boumediene overthrows Ben Bella. Boumediene's government takes ownership of industry and controls the economy.

1980 Government forces respond violently to a Berber student strike for political and cultural rights. Rioting leads to thirty-two deaths.

1984 The legislature adopts the Family Code, which makes women's legal status the same as children's in many areas of life.

1988 Marchers protest severe economic problems. Violence erupts, and President Bendjedid introduces a number of reforms.

1992 The military cancels elections to prevent an Islamist victory. Arrests and violent protests lead to the Algerian Civil War.

1993 Islamist extremists murder writer Tahar Djaout.

1999 The FIS agrees to a cease-fire. Voters approve an amnesty for rebels.

2000 The FIS disbands. Nouria Merah-Benida wins an Olympic gold medal for the women's 1,500-meter race.

2002 The legislature makes Berber a national language and adopts a National Environmental Action Plan.

2003 An earthquake kills and injures thousands. Extremists kidnap thirty-two European tourists. Berber-language instruction in schools begins.

2004 Voters reelect President Bouteflika in a landslide.

2005 Officials arrest the head of the extremist group, the GIA.

2006 Algeria hosts World Environment Day. A second amnesty for rebels becomes law. Musician Cheikha Remitti, the Queen of Raï, dies. Al-Qaeda joins with the Salafist terrorist group.

2007 Algeria continues to make progress on education and health care as it strives to meet the Millennium Development Goals by 2015.

COUNTRY NAME People's Democratic Republic of Algeria

AREA 919,595 square miles (2,381,740 sq. km)

MAIN LANDFORMS Ahaggar Mountains, Atlas Mountains (including Aurès Mountains, Kabylia Mountains, Saharan Atlas Mountains and Tell Atlas Mountains), Chech Erg, Chott Melrhir, Great Eastern Erg, Great Western Erg, High Plateau, Iguidi Erg, Medjerda range, Mzab plateau, Sahara, Tassili N'Ajjer Mountains

HIGHEST POINT Mount Tahat, 9,852 feet (3,003 m) above sea level

LOWEST POINT Chott Melrhir, 102 feet (31 m) below sea level

MAJOR RIVERS Chéliff, Seybouse, Soummam

ANIMALS Algerian nuthatch, anchovies, antelope, Audouin's gull, Barbary red deer, Barbary sheep, camels, cormorants, fennecs (desert fox), flamingos, gazelles, golden jackals, hares, hawks, jerboas, lammergeier, lizards, macaques (Barbary apes), Mediterranean monk seals, owls, porcupines, sand rats, sardines, scorpions, snakes, striped hyenas, terns, tuna, vultures, wild boars

CAPITAL CITY Algiers

OTHER MAJOR CITIES Annaba, Constantine, Oran

OFFICIAL LANGUAGE Arabic. Berber is the national language.

MONETARY UNIT Algerian dinar. 1 dinar = 100 centimes.

ALGERIAN CURRENCY

The Algerian dinar became Algeria's currency in 1963. It is made up of 100 centimes. Coins are available in 50, 20, 10, and 5 centimes amounts and 10, 5, and 1 dinar amounts. Notes, or paper money, are available in 1,000, 500, 200, 100, 50, 20, 10, and 5 dinar denominations. Scenes from Algeria's history decorate the colorful notes. They include the designs from ancient rock art, a pirate ship, and the Martyr's Monument in Algiers that honors independence fighters.

Algeria's early nationalist leader Ahmed Messali Hadj designed the nation's flag. The FLN adopted it as their flag in 1948, fourteen years before independence. The left (flagpole) half of the flag is green. The right half is white. The color white stands for purity. In the center of the flag, a red five-pointed star sits within a red crescent moon. The star, crescent, and the color green are traditional symbols of Islam. Many other Islamic nations use these elements in their flags. Green also symbolizes fertility.

Algeria adopted its national anthem upon independence from France in 1962. Mufdi Zakariah wrote the words while he was in prison under French rule. Mohamed Fawzi set the poem to music. An English translation follows below.

"Kassaman" (We Pledge)
We pledge by the lightning that destroys,
By the streams of generous blood being shed,
By the bright flags that wave,
Flying proudly on the high hills,
That we are in revolt, whether we live or die,
We are determined that Algeria should live,
So be our witness! Be our witness! Be our witness!

We are soldiers in revolt for truth,
And we have fought for our independence.
When we spoke, nobody listened to us,
So we have taken the noise of gunpowder as our rhythm
And the sound of machine guns as our melody,
We are determined that Algeria should live,
So be our witness! Be our witness! Be our witness!

For a link to a site where you can listen to Algeria's national anthem, "Kassaman," visit www.vgsbooks.com.

HASSIBA BOULMERKA (b. 1968) Hassiba Boulmerka is an Algerian track athlete, born in Constantine. In 1991 she became the first woman from an Arabic or African nation to win a World Track Championship. Muslim fundamentalists criticized her for running in what they considered to be immodest clothing. Boulmerka responded that while she was a practicing Muslim, she could not run in traditional dress, covered from head to toe. She became Algeria's first Olympic gold medalist in 1992, when she won the 1,500-meter race. An ankle injury in 1996 ended her professional running career.

ABDELAZIZ BOUTEFLIKA (b. 1937) Bouteflika became Algeria's president in 1999. Sources vary as to where he was born. He fought in Algeria's war against France. Afterward, he served as the foreign minister until 1979. Algeria's powerful military backed Bouteflika's 1999 bid for the presidency. As president, Bouteflika gave amnesty to Islamist forces that had been battling the government since 1992. His plan slowly brought some peace to Algeria. Promising to continue to build "true national reconciliation," Bouteflika won a second term in 2004. However, reports continue that his security forces abuse human rights.

ALBERT CAMUS (1913–1960) Camus was a pied-noir (French Algerian) writer. He won the Nobel Prize in Literature in 1957. Camus was born in Mondovi (modern Drean). His father was killed in World War I, and his mother worked as a housecleaner. Camus moved to France and joined the anti-Nazi movement during World War II. War, poverty, and illness were themes in his work. His philosophy of "the absurd" reflects his vision that humans suffer in a life that does not have meaning. Nevertheless, his heroes act with courage in the face of despair.

KAMAL DEHANE (b. 1954) Dehane is an Algerian filmmaker. Born in the first year of the Algerian Revolution, he witnessed the horrors of war as a child. He studied in Brussels, Belgium, and teaches filmmaking there. Dehane mostly makes documentaries. In his films such as *Women of Algiers* (1992), he addresses the plight of Algerian women and children. In 2004 Dehane's first fiction film, *The Suspects*, was about the crushing pressures of Algerian politics on a young man. He based it on the novel *The Watchers* by murdered author Tahar Djaout.

ASSIA DJEBAR (b. 1936) Assia Djebar is a novelist, scholar, poet, and filmmaker whose work focuses on women in Algeria. She was born Fatima Zohra Imalayen in Cherchell. Her writing has won many awards. Scholars consider her one of North Africa's most important authors. She is one of the few Algerian authors whose works are translated into English. In 2005 the French Academy (Académie Française), an elite cultural group in France, elected Djebar as a lifetime member. She is a professor at New York University.

LOUISA HANOUNE (b. 1954) Hanoune became the first Algerian woman to run for the presidency, in 2004. She leads the small Workers Party of Algeria. Born in Jibel, in eastern Algeria, to a peasant family, Hanoune became a lawyer who works for woman's rights. She supports a fully democratic process that includes radical Islamists.

KHALED (b. 1960) Born in Sidi-El-Houri, Khaled is a musician known as the King of Raï. His 2004 album, *Ya-Rahi* (Oh My!), merges Arab music with reggae, soul, and Latin American rock. Guitarist Carlos Santana joins Khaled on a song about hope, "Love to the People."

KHAYR AL-DIN (ca. 1483–1546) Khayr al-Din was a pirate and sea captain also known as Barbarossa, or Redbeard. He and his older brother Arouj al-Din organized a fleet of ships to roam the Mediterranean Sea. After his brother's death, Khayr al-Din captured Algiers in 1518 and placed it under the control of the Ottoman Turks. He became admiral of the Ottoman fleet in the western Mediterranean. He grew wealthy attacking European shipping and capturing thousands of prisoners for ransom.

NOUREDDINE MORCELI (b. 1970) Noureddine Morceli is one of Algeria's best track-and-field athletes. He won an Olympic gold medal in 1996 for the 1,500-meter race. A devout Muslim, he supported runner Hassiba Boulmerka in her struggles against Islamist harassment.

ABD AL-QADIR (ca. 1807–1883) Born in Muaskar, al-Qadir became an Algerian military leader and a Muslim religious leader. He set up his own government in opposition to French rule. The French defeated his guerrilla forces and sent him into exile. Al-Qadir devoted his final years to writing, before his death in Damascus, Syria. In 1970 his remains were returned to Algeria. He is still a national hero. For instance, raï musician Khaled recorded the song "Abdel Kader" (a spelling variation of Abd al-Qadir) to popular acclaim in 1998.

CHEIKHA REMITTI (1923–2006) Cheikha Remitti was a musician known as the Queen of Raï. As a girl in Relizane, she joined a traditional female dance troupe. She recorded her first song in 1936. Many of her songs relate the plight of women and celebrate pleasure and free love. She earned the name Cheikha (elder) with her tradition-based music, but she always looked to the future. She continued to perform until days before her death in Paris, France.

YVES SAINT-LAURENT (b. 1936) Saint-Laurent was born in Oran, Algeria, of French descent. When he was twenty-one, he became the head designer of the famous Dior fashion house in Paris, France. Four years later, he opened his own fashion house in Paris. He is one of the most influential fashion designers of the late twentieth century. He retired in 2002.

The U.S. Department of State warns that travel in Algeria is risky, especially in remote areas. If you're planning a trip, check the State Department's current travel warnings at http://www.travel.state.gov.

AIN SEFRA Called the Gateway to the Desert, this desert town sits where the Atlas Mountains descend into the Sahara. Ain Sefra offers views of rugged ridges, mountain gorges, and surrounding desert dunes. The town is also famous as the burial site of European writer Isabella Eberhardt, one of the great explorers of North Africa.

ALGIERS Most points of interest in Algeria's capital are found in the medina, or casbah quarter, built in the 1500s. Its dazzling white buildings start at the sea and rise steeply into the hills. The site of an old fortress crowns the hill. This walled area is Algiers's heart and has inspired movies, books, and music. Outside the casbah, visitors enjoy the Roman Catholic cathedral Our Lady of Africa; the Martyr's Monument, a memorial to the struggle for Algerian independence, where you can look out over the city; and the Grand Mosque. This is the city's oldest mosque, probably built in 1018. Columns joined by arches grace its beautiful interior.

EL-OUED Nicknamed the City of a Thousand Domes, El-Oued is the main town of the Souf area in the sand sea of the Great Eastern Erg. (*Souf* means "oasis.") Its desert architecture is picturesque—domed roofs on most buildings serve as shields against the burning sun. The town's carpets are famous for their traditional cross of the Souf—a brown cross on a pale background. Visitors buy them at the daily market in the old part of town. El-Oued is a good base to explore other villages of the region.

TASSILI N'AJJER NATIONAL PARK Located in Algeria's southeastern mountains, this park offers archaeological and natural wonders. It is the best place to see thousands of rock paintings and carvings that date back to 8000 B.C. In a famous engraving known as *The Crying Cows,* the cattle seem to come off the rock face toward the viewer. Wind erosion has carved rock arches, towers, and other dramatic landforms. The park's woodland is also home to endangered plants. Visitors need a permit and guide to visit this UN World Heritage Site.

TIPASA Algeria's Roman history is best viewed at Tipasa—a Phoenician trading post that became a Roman colony in the A.D. 100s. The well-preserved ruins of temples and other monuments can be seen, outlined against the Mediterranean Sea. Visitors walk among olive trees in the ancient forum. A small museum displays Roman relics. Prepare for a visit by reading the essay "Return to Tipasa" by Albert Camus.

Berbers: the native people of Algeria, also called Imazighen (Free People)

casbah: a North African fortress; the old section, or medina, of Algiers

colon: a European settler, usually French, in Algeria

desert: an area that receives less than 10 inches (25 cm) of rain a year

desertification: the process of dryland turning into desert, caused by human and climate factors. This is a major environmental challenge for Algeria.

FIS: Islamic Salvation Front (in French, Front Islamique du Salut). The government crackdown on the FIS party led to the outbreak of civil war in 1992.

FLN: National Liberation Front (in French, Front de Libération Nationale). Leaders of the Algerian Revolution, the FLN has dominated Algeria's government since independence.

gross domestic product (GDP): the value of goods and services produced in a country in a year

guerrilla war: fighting by small bands of rebels against government forces. Guerrillas use assassinations, bombings, hit-and-run strikes, and other terror tactics.

Islam: a religion founded through the Arab prophet Muhammad in the seventh century A.D. Followers are called Muslims. Sunni Islam is the religion's largest branch.

literacy: the ability to read and write a basic sentence

mosque: an Islamic place of worship and prayer

nationalist: a patriot, or person who wants independence for his or her nation

nomads: herders who move with their animals in search of pasture and water

oasis: a fertile place in the desert where underground water comes to or near the surface

pieds-noirs: French colons (colonists) and their descendants in Algeria

Quran: the holy book of Islam. The prophet Muhammad dictated the book starting in A.D. 610. Muslims believe these scriptures come from God.

souk: an open-air marketplace. Modern souks offer everything from live chicken to DVDs.

Glossary

BBC News. 2006.
http://www.bbc.co.uk (June 2006).
The World Edition of the BBC (British Broadcasting Corporation) News is updated throughout the day, every day. The BBC is a source for comprehensive news coverage about Algeria and also provides a country profile.

Central Intelligence Agency (CIA). "Algeria." *The World Factbook.* 2006.
http://www.cia.gov/cia/publications/factbook/geos/ag.html (May 2006).
This CIA website provides facts and figures on Algeria's geography, people, government, economy, communications, transportation, military, and more.

Ciment, James. *Algeria: The Fundamentalist Challenge.* New York: Facts on File, 1997.
The author, a professor of history, discusses the forces within Algeria that led to the civil war that engulfed the nation beginning in 1992.

Coulson, David. "Ancient Art of the Sahara." *National Geographic,* June 1999, 98–120.
Rock art in Algeria's Tassili N'Ajjer Mountains have survived the elements for thousands of years. This article tells the story and documents the art in beautiful photographs.

Cutter, Charles H. *Africa 2005.* Harpers Ferry, WV: Stryker-Post, 2005.
The article on Algeria in this annual volume of the World Today series provides a moderately detailed look at recent culture, politics, and economics.

Diagram Group. *History of North Africa.* New York: Facts on File, 2003.
Part of the Peoples of Africa series, this book clearly presents historical information essential to understanding North Africa's recent political history.

Economist. 2006.
http://www.economist.com (May 2006)
A weekly British magazine, the *Economist* provides coverage of Algeria's political and economic news. The *Economist* also offers country profiles with relevant articles as well as some statistics at http://www.economist.com/countries.

Gordon, Matthew. *Islam.* Rev. ed. New York: Facts on File, 2001.
This book, part of the World Religions series, provides an overview of Islam. It discusses the religion's history, basic beliefs, and the modern Islamic world.

Library of Congress—Federal Research Division. *Country Profile: Algeria.* March 2006.
http://lcweb2.loc.gov/frd/cs/profiles/Algeria.pdf (June 2006)
This updated profile presents information about Algeria's geography, society, economy, government, and more. The complete *Country Study: Algeria* (1994) is also available at http://lcweb2.loc.gov/frd/cs/dztoc.html.

Lindqvist, Sven. *Desert Divers.* New York: Granta Books, 2002.
This book is an imaginative look at foreigners' love affair with the desert and their exploitation of the Sahara. Lindqvist writes of historical travelers and his own travels in the Maghreb.

Middle East and North Africa, 2006. **London: Routledge, 2005.**
This annual volume is part of the Europa Regional Surveys of the World. Its long section on Algeria covers the country's recent history, geography, economy, and culture. Statistics and sources are included.

Naylor, Phillip Chiviges, and Alf Andrew Heggoy. ***The Historical Dictionary of Algeria.*** **2nd ed. Metuchen, NJ: Scarecrow Press, 1994.**
A very useful reference book, this dictionary includes short articles on culture, economics, history, politics, and social issues, as well as informative entries on people, places, and events.

Population Reference Bureau. **2005.**
http://www.prb.org (May 2006).
PRB's annual statistics provide in-depth demographics on Algeria's population, including birthrates and death rates, infant mortality rates, and other statistics relating to health, environment, education, employment, and more.

Rogerson, Barnaby. ***A Traveller's History of North Africa.*** **Brooklyn: Interlink Books, 1998.**
This book covers Morocco, Tunisia, Libya, and Algeria—countries with shared, as well as individual, history. The complex cultural background of the region, with its many peoples and conquerors, is woven with a colorful cast of characters in this very readable history. It covers prehistoric times to the late twentieth century.

Sukys, Julija. ***Silence Is Death: The Life and Work of Tahar Djaout.*** **Lincoln and London: University of Nebraska Press, 2007.**
This biography looks at the life of the Algerian novelist, poet, and journalist who was assassinated in 1993.

University of Pennsylvania, African Studies Center. **"Algeria." 2007.**
http://www.sas.upenn.edu/African_Studies/Country_Specific/Algeria.html (January 2007).
The African Studies Center offers many links to resources to find information about Algeria.

U.S. Department of State, Bureau of African Affairs. ***Background Note: Algeria.*** **2006.**
http://www.state.gov/r/pa/ei/bgn/8005.htm (May 9, 2006).
The background notes of the U.S. State Department supplies a profile of Algeria's people, history, government, economy, and more.

Weatherby, Joseph N. ***The Middle East and North Africa: A Political Primer.*** **New York: Longman, 2002.**
An overview of the forces that shape the part of the world that includes Algeria: land and water issues, a history of colonialism by foreign powers, the culture and politics of religion, and more.

World Health Organization (WHO). ***Algeria.*** **June 30, 2006.**
http://www.who.int/countries/dza/en/index.html (July 2006).
The World Health Organization is the United Nations specialized agency for health. WHO's country page for Algeria links to detailed information on selected health topics and statistics. It also links to information about specific diseases, such as plague.

Algeria: Information and Destination Guide
http://www.algeria.com
This BBC-recommended site offers a wealth of culture, news, and travel information.

Algeria Daily
http://www.algeriadaily.com/
This site provides Algerian news in English from sources around the world, gathered by World News Network.

Ayoub, Abderrahman, and others. *Umm El Madayan: An Islamic City Through the Ages*. Boston: Houghton Mifflin, 1994.
Umm El Madayan means the "Mother of Cities" in Arabic. It is a fictional city representing any of many cities on Algeria's Mediterranean coast. Finely detailed pen drawings by Francesco Corni wonderfully illustrate the book. They show the historical, architectural, and cultural development of the city as it evolves from a hunting-gathering site, to a Phoenician colony, to a Roman, then Arab city, and so on, up to the twenty-first century.

Camus, Albert. *The Plague*. Translated by Stuart Gilbert. New York: Viking, 1991.
This novel was first published in France as *La Peste* in 1947. Trouble begins in this famous novel with the main character noticing a dead rat lying on the staircase. The rat signals a plague epidemic, and the city (Oran) is closed. It becomes like a laboratory, testing how humans behave in the face of suffering. Camus said that the story, written in the World War II era, represented the European struggle against Nazi Germany.

Diagram Group. *Peoples of North Africa*. New York: Facts on File, 1997.
This book is part of the Peoples of Africa series. It presents the different cultures and traditions of the major ethnic groups of North Africa, including the Berbers and Arabs of Algeria.

Djaout, Tahar. *The Last Summer of Reason*. Translated by Marjolijn de Jager. Saint Paul: Ruminator Books, 2001.
This short novel tells the story of a lonely bookseller. He lives in a country being taken over by religious fundamentalists. They outlaw music, burn books, and put up warning signs, such as "Woe to a people who let things be run by a woman." The haunting story is an allegory (symbolic tale) for any society where intolerance limits human freedoms. Opponents of Djaout's views assassinated the author before this book was published.

Feraoun, Mouloud. *Journal, 1955–1962: Reflections on the French-Algerian War*. Edited by James D. Le Sueur. Lincoln: University of Nebraska Press, 2000.
This is a firsthand account of the Algerian Revolution by Feraoun—an Algerian teacher and writer who asks, "Can words express the horror that grips us?" Feraoun's journal ends abruptly in 1962—a group of French colon extremists murdered him.

Graffenried, Michael, von. *Inside Algeria.* New York: Aperture, 1998. Introduction "Life and Death in Algeria" by Mary-Jane Deeb.

Swiss photographer von Graffenried photographed conflict and daily life in Algeria during the violent 1990s. He worked secretly, with a hidden camera, because the Islamic terrorists had executed more than sixty journalists and photographers. His notes explain the powerful black-and-white photos.

Jelloun, Tahar Ben. *Islam Explained.* Toronto: University of Toronto Press, 2004.

This is a clear introduction to the history and main beliefs of Islam. Presented in question-and-answer format between the author and young questioners, the book also defines words often heard in the news, such as *terrorist* and *fundamentalist*. It is a useful book for anyone who wants to learn about Islam in modern times.

Pontecorvo, Gillo. *The Battle of Algiers.* DVD. Criterion Collection, 2004.

The Algerian government commissioned this famous 1967 film. It is a documentary-like fictional look at Algeria's war against France. Director Pontecorvo shows the bloody struggle from both sides. The moviemaker shows their clash, contrasting the French use of torture with the Algerians' use of bombs in public places. This three-DVD release includes documentaries and interviews about the historic movie.

Swift, Jeremy. *The Sahara.* Amsterdam: Time-Life Books, 1975.

This title offers a natural, scientific, and cultural history of the Sahara. The author has done broad research in the Sahara, including living with Tuareg herders there. The accompanying photographs of the desert landscape are awe inspiring.

United Nations Statistics Division. *Millenium Development Goals: Algeria.*
http://mdgs.un.org/unsd/mdg/Data.aspx?cr=12 (November 2006)

The United Nations tracks countries' progress with the eight Millennium Development Goals outlined in 2000. This site provides statistics for Algeria's MDG progress. It also links to the home page, which offers more links to MDG information.

vgsbooks.com
http://www.vgsbooks.com

Visit vgsbooks.com, the home page of the Visual Geography Series®, which is updated regularly. You can get linked to all sorts of useful online information, including geographical, historical, demographic, cultural, and economic websites. The vgsbooks.com site is a great resource for late-breaking news and statistics.

Winget, Mary, and Habib Chalbi. *Cooking the North African Way.* Minneapolis: Lerner Publications Company, 2004.

The cuisines of North Africa—Morocco, Algeria, Tunisia, Libya, and Egypt—are featured in this cultural cookbook. Besides offering a wide sampling of recipes, this book looks at the land and customs of the region.

Captions for photos appearing on cover and chapter openers:

Cover: Nomads herd their sheep in the Sahara against a backdrop of sand dunes.

pp. 4–5 Algeria boasts a beautiful Mediterranean coast in addition to mountains, plateaus, and the Sahara.

pp. 8–9 Sand dunes rise above a village in the Sahara. People settle around oases, which provide much-needed water in the desert.

pp. 20–21 Carvings on rock can be found throughout the Tassili N'Ajjer Mountains in southeastern Algeria. Some of the art is up to ten thousand years old and shows images of humans and animals.

pp. 38–39 In Algeria's capital city of Algiers, on the Mediterranean seacoast, people dress in traditional clothes and Western-style clothing. Much of Algeria's population resides in coastal cities.

pp. 48–49 Algerians are known for their ceramics, pottery, and silverwork.

pp. 58–59 Women and men look over produce at an open-air market in a suburb of Algiers.